Fly Fishing California's Great Waters

Dan Blanton

Fly Fishing
California's
Great Waters

Dan Blanton

Frank
Amato
PORTLAND

Dedication

I dedicate this book to my wife, Cindy, my best friend, my partner in life and always an inspiration. She has always supported my outdoors career in the most positive way, giving solid advice when asked for and also knowing when not to offer it—good partners just know these things. She's kind, warm and most of all patient. Without her encouragement and support I know I wouldn't be where I am today. I certainly wouldn't be as successful and most importantly, as happy with my life as I am. I am indeed, blessed.

Special Thanks

I would like to extend special thanks to my dearest, life-long friend and mentor, Lefty Kreh, who over the past 35 years has been a caring, sharing friend and advisor, one who influenced me more than anyone I know. Much of the best of what I know about writing and photography has come from the tutelage of Lefty. Thanks old friend.

I would also like to thank Jim Schollmeyer and Dave Hughes for continuously encouraging me to write a book and for giving me the idea for this book. They were tenacious, hounding me like old fish wives to get it done. Thanks guys, you can let up now. Thanks too, to my old compadre, Ken Hanley for his long support and friendship and for writing such a wonderful Foreword for this book. Muchas gracias amigo!

© 2003 Dan Blanton

Frank Amato Publications, Inc.
P.O. Box 82112, Portland, Oregon 97282
503.653.8108 • www.amatobooks.com

All photographs by the author unless otherwise noted.
Book & Cover Design: Kathy Johnson
Printed in Singapore
Softbound ISBN: 1-57188-289-8 • UPC: 0-81127-00118-7
Hardbound ISBN: 1-57188-292-8 • UPC: 0-81127-00122-4
Limited Edition ISBN: 1-57188-293-6

1 3 5 7 9 10 8 6 4 2

Contents

FOREWORD

6

INTRODUCTION

8

1 CHAPTER

King of the
North Coast Rivers

10

2 CHAPTER

San Francisco Bay:
The Middle Ground

16

3 CHAPTER

California Delta:
New Home Waters

22

4 CHAPTER

Largemouth Bass
Wonderland

30

5 CHAPTER

Monterey Bay
Potpourri

38

6 CHAPTER

The Return of
Monterey Bay
White Sea Bass

46

7 CHAPTER

A Legacy of Blues

52

8 CHAPTER

Lakes of Giants

56

9 CHAPTER

Nacimiento Whites

64

10 CHAPTER

Fall River Valley:
Trout Opportunities
From a Fast Boat

70

11 CHAPTER

Spring Fever Shad

76

12 CHAPTER

Great Flies for
Great Waters

82

INDEX

88

Foreword

A selection of typical western shad flies. This is a popular style but shad flies can also be tied unweighted and without bead eyes.

Man, does time fly! I can still remember the first time I read one of Dan's articles on San Francisco Bay stripers. Let's just say that it was many decades ago. His writing was the catalyst for opening up a whole new angling world for me—right in my own backyard.

Over the years I followed Dan's adventures, through numerous articles and speaking engagements at clubs and sports shows. In every instance he never failed to inspire me. I explored new waters. I tried new field techniques. I loved the process and indeed enjoyed some angling success. He soon became a mentor in my flyfishing career, always gracious with a seemingly endless resource of valuable information.

As I entered the professional flyfishing arena, Dan was again a source of inspiration and camaraderie. I value his friendship. I truly admire his passion. His perspective on the flyfishing experience is grounded in "water time." The guy is constantly

working on perfecting his field techniques with hands-on experience. His observations on equipment selection and design come from actual use under demanding angling conditions. He's been there—you can count on it!

Fly Fishing California's Great Waters is a treasure chest of practical information. You'll gain insights into specific locations, seasonal details, and the natural history of game fish, equipment selection, and field applications. In addition, there's plenty of historical reference to the anglers and individuals responsible for broadening the flyfishing tapestry of the Golden State. Dan's respect for the folks who've pioneered our sport is a recognizable trademark in his writing style. Having personally shared the water with many of these legends, his storytelling originates from an insider's view. Go ahead and make a quick check into the bountiful literature of our sport, you're sure to find Dan's own fingerprints throughout the fresh and saltwater worlds of fly-fishing.

Above: A fat San Luis striper taken on a blue anchovy Sar-Mul-Mac.

Below: Left to right: Foam Swimming Hex Emerger, Quigley's Cripple, Hex dry.

Dan and I have had the pleasure of travelling together and exploring a variety of fisheries from silver salmon in British Columbia, to false albacore in North Carolina. Yet, our conversations inevitably would turn back to our home waters of California. Simply put, we have an amazing state for flyfishing adventures. Dan knows this. He believes this. So do I. You will too, once you take the opportunity to use Dan's book as a catalyst to experience some of California's "great waters." I'm sure of it!

cheers,
Ken Hanley

Introduction

Smith River legend,
Ted Linder nets a heavy king on the
Smith River's Piling Hole (circa 1970).

o adequately write about all of California's great flyfishing waters would take volumes. I've always maintained that any fly-fisher who really wanted to sample all of the great fresh- or saltwater fly-fishing throughout the state would have to become a fishing bum, pursuing their passion to the exclusion of family, friends and career—there's that much of it, year-round. He or she would also have to have a keen desire to be diverse, to learn reams of information about various fisheries, their game species and the techniques needed to catch them—when, where and how—and their flyfishing skills would have to be finely honed. A willingness to breach convention would also be a requirement.

During my long career as a fly-angler, writer and outdoorsman, I've been graced with the opportunity to chase fly-eating game fish the world over, sampling some of this planet's most appealing angling Meccas. My broad traveling experiences have brought me to the conclusion that California offers some of the best in fly-angling destinations to be found anywhere—great waters—and it would take a lifetime to sample them all in such a way as to be able to say you knew them well.

This book is a collection of stories I've written for various flyfishing periodicals over the decades. It details only 11 of many great waters, ones I've come to know and love during the past 45 years of passionate flyfishing. No, I didn't become a flyfishing bum, as several of my friends and associates did, but I could have easily gone that route. The opportunity and motivating factors were certainly there. Instead I picked a handful of shining fisheries to learn well and write about, all of which ultimately became my favorite California great waters. Two became my "home waters"—San Francisco Bay and the California delta—the latter of which contains a thousand miles of meandering, backcountry waterways, teaming with the likes of striped bass, largemouth bass, salmon and other wonderful fly-rod fish. I've spent countless hours there, and I'm still learning and marveling at this incredible angling wonderland. I am forever grateful to my friend, Jay Remley who introduced me to this remarkable resource.

Each chapter provides insight into the fishery, some history, and of course all the whens, wheres and hows based on my personal experience. I've told a tale or two about a couple of angling legends, such as the late Bill Schaadt a marvelous angler and person, someone I liked and respected and truly miss not seeing on the water or at an angling exposition. Pulling old photographs of Bill to illustrate Chapter 1: Kings of the North Coast Rivers, brought back many fond memories of the "legend" and wonderful times shared on those incredible rivers. I've provided the publisher with my best photography to illustrate the book. They cover the decades and I believe you will enjoy them as much as I do, along with the many insights they provide to these great waters. Some chapters contain sidebar information encapsulating certain pertinent information, placing it at your fingertips. Others won't because it wasn't needed.

Chapter 12: Great Flies for Great Waters discusses just what the title suggests and provides a photo-

The late Bill Schaadt was always in the "meat bucket" and was considered to be the finest salmon and steelhead fly-fisherman to ever wet a line in the north coast rivers.

graphic illustrations of what I consider to be the best fly patterns or "styles" for each of the 11 great waters. Many of the flies are what I refer to as "crossover" patterns, meaning they will produce in both fresh and saltwater for a variety of species. These are the best of the best, and you won't often fail using them.

Fly Fishing California's Great Waters is my first book and I feel confident that reading it will engender a spirit of adventure and a desire to give all these great waters and fish a try—or at least most of them. If you already have tested all or some of these waters, you're bound to learn something new or at least discover another "right" way of doing it. Enjoy!

Kings of the North Coast

The line-up builds quickly, well before the sun rises. Be on the water early if you want a good spot. Inset: An electric trolling motor is very useful when you have to chase down a fish.

The fall equinox marks a time of profound change. Northcoast forests become garnished with brilliant swaths of color—reds, yellows, oranges and purples. The scent of fir hangs heavy in damp air. River pools, low, crystalline and earlier devoid of salmon, begin to fill with long, dark shapes, salmon, thick across the shoulders. Days are shorter, but warm, often hot; while nights are cool and crisp, turning morning exhales into wisps of steam, the chilled air biting the ears, noses and lips of pre-dawn fishermen. For some, thoughts sway from trout, bass or stripers, to salmon—North coast river salmon; and Sunday drives through local redwood groves stir nostalgia, filling one's mind with images of successful yesterdays—battles with heavy chinooks, Kings of the North Coast Rivers. Anxiety piques and plans are quickly set for excursions north by veteran salmon anglers; destinations: the Smith or Chetco rivers, two of the best when it comes to fly-fishing for big, river-run king salmon.

The Smith River

The Smith River, coursing its way through dark forests and steep-sided canyons, shimmering like a gilded ribbon on its way to sea, is one of the last un-dammed watercourses remaining in California. Having it harnessed would mean the end of a legend, for more fly-caught king salmon exceeding 50 pounds have come from the Smith River than from any other in the lower 48. It is one of the fastest-clearing streams after a pelting storm, often fishable within 24 hours.

Noting exceptions, salmon usually enter the system in fishable numbers beginning about the third week of October, peaking around the end of the first week of November; although superb angling some years has lasted until after Thanksgiving, depending upon the weather. Like much fishing, weather has the lead role as a determining factor. A hot bite can be stifled by a rising river only to resume again a few days following a passing storm. Being able to flex angling time increases the chances for a successful salmon season on north coast salmon streams.

Piling Hole, Rowdy Creek Hole, Woodruff, Baily, Buck Early, Peacock, Society, Hiuchi Bridge Hole, the Park Hole, Water Gauge—all familiar names to those who covet the Smith. They are holes which have all produced phenomenal fly-rod catches during the last 50 years. Could they talk, they would tell stories of fish and fishermen that would tantalize your angling sensitivities beyond belief. Attempting to suggest which of these are best, or even where to begin, would be extremely difficult, if not foolhardy. No one can accurately predict where the fish will hold from season to season.

The Chetco River

At one time, Oregon's Chetco River, located just across the California/Oregon border where it empties into the ocean at Brookings, produced salmon averaging much smaller than those found in the Smith River. This is no longer true due to the efforts of the Oregon Department of Fish and Wildlife. As a result of introducing Smith River salmon strains and others to the Chetco River, the size of its average salmon now rival those of the Smith. Fish exceeding 60 pounds are now taken yearly from the Chetco.

Like the Smith, the best beats on the Chetco are often the pools in the lower section—Tide Rock, Morris and Snug Harbor, for example. However, great fly-fishing can exist as far upriver as 8 to 15 miles, depending upon conditions. Unless you have gotten the word from someone knowledgeable, your first day on these rivers might be best spent reconnoitering.

The author with a big Smith River king salmon (circa 1970).

Left: Anglers fly-fishing the lower Smith River at Piling Hole.

Many Skills Are Required

Fly-rodding for river king salmon California/Oregon style, requires the angler, in my opinion, to have more combined skills than any other type of freshwater fly-fishing. Ditto for many of the saltwater venues as well.

To consistently take kings on a fly, the angler must first locate the fish by exploring the river pools: driving the river roads, stopping at holes which his-torically hold fish to watch for signs of them—rolling

salmon, a lineup of anglers, anglers doing battle. Locating fish is not always as easy as this sounds. Some pools can't be seen from the road and must be walked to. Locating productive holes can be difficult for neophytes, and even if you can find the best pools, the fish often don't show for one reason or another. Don't count on anglers fishing the pools to always give you a clue, some can be pretty sly about not advertising the fact the hole is loaded.

Once a concentration of fish is located, the next step is to ascertain where in the pool the largest mass of fish are holding or where they are making a turn, an area affectionately called the "meat bucket or bucket." This will be the most productive area of the pool. As the late, legendary Bill Schaadt once said, "One cast into the bucket is worth ten that are out of it!" "If you're not in the bucket you might as well be in the parking lot!" Getting into the bucket can be a tough chore, particularly if you have arrived late.

After locating fish and determining where in the pool the meat bucket is, you'll have to launch your pram (there is very little wade-fishing available) sometimes two hours before dawn to be sure of getting a top spot, often having to row across a stout current and often long distances. Determining just the right place to drop the hook for positioning the boat in the dark is not an easy task for the inexperienced.

Getting on the water early, before the lineup forms, is the easy way. Working into an established lineup, however, which is often a gunnel-to-gunnel situation and then properly anchoring so the boat will hold in the current without disturbing others, can require extreme skill and diplomacy. Knowing a lot of people helps, too. Sometimes you'll anchor stern to the fish, other times it's gunnel to them, depending upon conditions. Two anchors are almost always required.

Once anchored, the angler needs to determine which density shooting head will best take the fly to the level of the fish, and then what retrieval pattern will score best. While a great variety of fly patterns such as comet and shrimp styles work most of the time, kings can often lock on to a particular color or pattern, refusing all others. Be observant and ask the right questions. Once settled with all the right stuff, most anglers cast while standing, since long casts are often required. You'll need both good sea legs and casting skills.

Hook a fish and you'll need to determine if it's fair-hooked or fouled, since a lot of salmon are foul-hooked unintentionally and should be immediately broken off. Fouled king salmon usually zip off in a series of frenzied leaps, while fair-hooked fish usually hold and shake their head violently, trying to throw the fly before making a run for it. The head shaking can be felt in a bucking rod tip, but you can be sometimes fooled by a tail shake. If the fish is fair but can't be fought from the anchored position, which is often the case, you'll have to pull anchors using one hand while holding the rod with the other. Some shove the rod between their legs and use both hands for anchor hauling and rowing out of the line-up. I once saw a guy holding the rod in his teeth while pulling anchors and rowing out. Hey, whatever works!

Finally, once out of the line-up you'll have to fight a strong, heavy fish, one that will tow your pram all over the pool, which means you'll have to alternate between rowing and doing battle. Most of the fighting is done while standing and one needs to be careful not to be knocked out of the boat by the ores; or to lose one's balance and topple out. Rolling the boat is a distinct possibility, too. I find the use of an electric motor on my pram markedly helpful.

You'll have to force the fish out of the pool, if possible, in order that others may continue to fish; and you'll often have to untangle crossed lines—some with fish attached, and not always belonging to other fly-fishers. I've seen as many as six prams with fly-rodders doing battle while simultaneously occupying the same arena. Wild!

To locate pools holding salmon, drive the river roads looking for line-ups of prams and anglers fighting fish. Once you locate a hole holding fish, plan on being there before daylight the next morning.

Above: Mike Lawfler with a Smith River 50-pounder.

If you can beat the critter afloat, you'll have to net it using one hand. If the fish can't be netted from the boat or if it is more prudent to beach it, then you'll have to row to shore while fighting and towing the fish, this is not easy when there is a stiff current. More than one angler has found himself slipping over the edge of a riffle or rapid while doing battle from the boat—yours truly included.

The rule of the river is: when an angler leaves the line-up with a hooked fish, the spot vacated is his or hers again upon return. However it is acceptable to 'borrow' a spot while the angler is fighting the salmon. Be prepared, though, for the angler's friends to remind you that the position is not yours to keep. I have done this on numerous occasions and have hooked fished during the period in which the original occupant was gone.

Regardless of the techniques involved or which style one uses to accomplish all of this, it is going to take a great deal of skill and dexterity. This is a one-on-one situation—fly angler against salmon—with little help coming from anyone else. You are in the "arena" and must deal with it solo the vast majority of the time.

Social Fishing

Fly-fishing for Smith and Chetco river kings, including many other California/Oregon streams, is social fishing at its pinnacle. If you're a fly-fisher who prefers solitude, dislikes the constant drum of angling rhetoric, or lacks the confidence to go into the arena, as Bill Schaadt called it, then this, indeed, is not for you.

For a great many though, myself included, we look forward to the annual fall gathering on the Smith and Chetco rivers—the gathering of salmon and fly anglers alike. Today the event is almost like a conclave. Fly-rodders converge upon these watersheds from all over the

west, seeking kings, old friends and camaraderie. We fish together, share the experiences of the day, those of seasons past, and tell tales of great fly-rod fish taken elsewhere. For many old friends, its the only time of year we get to visit with each other. And, we catch salmon, king salmon on a fly.

Many people ask, how can you stand fishing in that crowd? Well, Bill Schaadt's response is my favorite. When asked that question once, Bill looked the angler straight in the eye and said, "It's only crowded on the surface..."

Usually there is considerable cooperation among these river fly-rodders. Tolerance is the key. We have to tolerate close fishing, adverse conditions and sometimes abrasive personalities. We know that to beef amongst ourselves, or with those fishing from the bank with bait or conventional gear, will only make matters worse. So most of us make a concerted effort to get along. If we do have problems, it is usually with newcomers, folks that don't know the rules of the game, fly-rodders who don't realize that a six-foot space between prams means there is room for one more boat.

I can recall on more than one occasion getting on the water late, possibly my first day on the river, only to find the line-up so tight I'd need a crowbar to get in. Still, after rowing around a little, an old friend like Al Perryman or Bill Schaadt would give me subtle nod to row over and squeeze in. More often than not I'd be in the bucket. Of course I've reciprocated on numerous occasions.

I can recall once when Rich Hutcherson's was the only boat in a bucket so tight that two friends anchored up behind him and cast over his head in order to get their flies into the fish. It worked and they all caught fish.

A Helping Hand

During the late sixties and seventies, old-timers like Pete Valconesi, Marty Medin, Terry Wallings, Bob Edgley, Lawrence Summers, Ben Miller, and Doc Bergmann, just to name a few, would pull out of a line-up, row up to the bow of a boat in which an angler was fighting a fish, drop their anchor into the guy's boat and then tow angler and boat out of the hole and to shore while the angler fought the fish. They would usually only do this for anglers who appeared to be having difficulty yanking a big fish out of the hole. We figured it was better to have one guy out of it for a while, instead of the entire group.

Fly-rodders weren't the only ones helped. I remember a particular day on the Smith's Park hole. A young kid fishing from the high rock had hooked a big fish on bait gear and was having a hell of a time with it. He was tying up the hole and some of the fly-fishermen were

Top: The Smith River has produced many 50-pound-plus king salmon on fly. Ed Given of Salinas, California displays his first 50-pounder (circa 1974).

starting to give the boy a hard time. Well, the late Tiny Blakely, a boisterous but great old-time Smith River fly-rodder, who had a heart as big as the 10-foot pram he fished out of, rowed over, picked up the kid and dared anyone to give him any crap as he chauffeured the boy around the pool for the next hour and a half (Tiny wasn't tiny). The youngster landed the fish, thanks to Blakely. It topped 60 pounds. Today bankers are still given a ride now and then if need be.

It Wasn't Always That Way...

Conversely, during the early days, Smith River fly-fishermen weren't quite so cooperative, and were a lot more secretive. They felt they had to be. This great sport of fly-rodding for massive king salmon was relatively new and only a few were participating or knew anything about it. It was indeed, an esoteric sport. They really wanted to keep it to themselves. I can't say I blame them.

In fact, I recall Bob Nauheim, who wrote the first article for *Outdoor Life* about fly-fishing for Smith River kings, telling me that he had asked Russ Chatham if he thought a story would bring hordes to the Smith. Chatham's reply was something like: "No way, Bob, this fishing is just too obscure!" Bob wrote the article, what was once obscure was no longer, and the hordes came. Russ was wrong.

It wasn't other fly-rodders they were particularly concerned about, it was the bank anglers—"rock turkeys" as we called them—the bait and hardware fishermen, many of them great anglers in their own right. The problem was that the two methods of angling just didn't mix well. They still don't. If the fly-boys found a hole with a bunch of fish in it, they'd do their best to keep it a secret.

I vividly recall the first time I met and saw Bill Schaadt in action. He was fishing the Smith's Cable hole with Bob Nauheim. It was around 1968 and Bob Edgley, Lawrence Summers and I had been drifting the river looking for fish. When we drifted into the Cable hole, Bill Schaadt was fighting a whopper, so we pulled our prams onto the bar, got out and watched. Bill was wade-fishing. He didn't seem to mind us, he knew Bob and Lawrence, but when two guys walked up and peered over the high bank, Bill tucked his rod under his left arm, pulled out his handkerchief, blew his nose, stuffed the rag back in his pocket and proceeded to shoot the breeze with us as though nothing were happening. He did this for 15 or 20 minutes (salmon tugging on his line the entire time) until the two observers left. Nauheim stayed on the bank talking with us. I don't think the pair was ever the wiser.

I learned later from Bob Nauheim that only a day or so after the handkerchief bit on the same pool, Schaadt suggested they stop fishing, go to the bank and eat their sandwiches when a few lookers poked their heads over the high bank. "Bob," said Schaadt, "people love watching people fish, but people hate watching people eat their lunch."

Bill had a lot of tricks, some of them scurrilous. His most famous, or infamous, one was the Razor Blade Fly. Bill, indeed had a Razor Blade Fly. A large, number-two, Gold Comet with a razor blade brazed to it, running at an angle between the hook-shank and barb. He only used it in desperation when bait fishermen would constantly cast into the middle of the pool with heavy sinkers, bottom fishing, completely cutting off all of a fly-rodder's drift. Or, when someone wouldn't break off a fouled fish. One sweep through the pool with the Razor Fly...oh well, you get the picture.

Back then a lot of the locals were pretty helpful to the few fly-rodders that plied the river. They weren't a threat to them then. In fact, Nauheim learned of the Cable hole through one of the local bait fishermen. It was loaded with big fish. After getting the word, Bob took a 48- and 49-pounder in consecutive days from the Cable hole. Schaadt took a 52-pounder. Bob took his first Cable hole fish by roll-casting from the high bank. It weighed 42 pounds and he recalls it being tough work hauling it up the steep bank.

River of Giants

As mentioned earlier, the Smith River has produced more fly-caught King salmon exceeding 50 pounds than all the others combined. The late Bill Schaadt certainly took his share of them, his largest a 57 1/2-pounder.

Others who have taken their half-century fish on a fly from the Smith include such anglers as: Bob Edgley with his 50-pounder, Ed Given with a 54 1/2-pounder, and yours truly with a 54 1/2-pound king that took me an hour and ten minutes to land on 10-pound tippet. That fish got me first place in the annual 1971 *Field & Stream* fishing contest, fly-rod division. At the time it was the second largest king ever taken on a fly. Schaadt's was the largest.

Fly Fishing California's Great Waters

The Marathon Fish

There have been great fish to remember, but even Schaadt's 57 1/2-pounder isn't the one he remembers best. The one he remembered most vividly up until the time of his death, was the one he fought for 11 hours, believing—convinced—all the while it was the long sought-after 60-pounder. Everyone fishing the hole, including Bill, thought it was the one and Bill admits he got psyched out hoping he would be the first to take a 60-pound king on a fly and backed the heat way down. When the salmon was brought to hand it was found to weight only 49 pounds—not the coveted 60-pounder everyone hoped and prayed it was; and, believe it or not, was a fish that Bill had fought, landed and released only a few days before. How did he know this particular salmon was the same fish? He knew because he had released it by quickly popping the leader, leaving his fly in the

bass fishing, but quickly found a use for it on the Smith and Chetco rivers and it became one of the most important lines when the river was up. Ironically, Gregory never fished for kings on either of these two remarkable watercourses.

Beginning in the late sixties and through the early

Upper right: Not the marathon fish but a good one that took Bill Schaadt more than an hour to land. He took the fish on 8-pound tippet and a size-10 fly (circa 1989).

Middle: It pays to have a large selection of flies in a variety of colors, styles and sizes.

Lower left: A large net is required and you'll have to learn to net a big fish with one hand while holding on to the rod with the other and keeping your balance.

corner of the king's massive maw. The marathon fish at Schaadt's feet wore both of his flies, one in each corner of its mouth. It was one of the few real disappointments of Bill's long and wondrous angler career.

The Right Lines

The very earliest Smith River fly-rod pioneers, guys like Schaadt, Jack Geib, Grant King, Doc Bergman, Ted Linder, Jack Horner and others, didn't have all the modern fly lines anglers have at their disposal today. There was only the Dacron shooting-head made by the Sunset Line & Twine Co., and the lead-core heads that were home-made at the time. Bill Schaadt was introduced to the lead-core head by Myron Gregory for Pacific kelp

seventies a proliferation of shooting-tapers in varying densities where developed by leading line makers at the urging of western salmon and steelhead fly-anglers. These lines allow north coast salmon fly-fishers to ply the entire water column, regardless of conditions. Lines ranging from intermediate densities for low-water conditions, to type 7 sinking and lead-core densities for use on deep pools or when the river is up and turbid. Yes, indeed, the smart angler still carries the lead line. Most anglers still prefer a mono-type shooting line which permits great distance, depth and sensitivity.

We have the best of graphite rods, and state-of-the-art reels, too. But most importantly, we still have big, tough and challenging salmon running up the Smith and Chetco rivers during the fall equinox. These may well be the toughest freshwater fish to catch on a fly—the Kings of the North Coast Rivers—and they're yours to take a shot at, but only if you are willing to be on the water early, work hard, fish smart and be sociable.

San Francisco Bay:
The Middle Ground

Schoolie action on the Middle Ground of San Francisco Bay, angler John Ryzanich fights and lands one.

Inset: Author displays a schoolie as his dog, Casey, looks on.

I t had been one of those rare and wonderful late-September days on San Francisco Bay. John Ryzanych and I had been on the water since before dawn and it was approaching that "magic" time—the last of the incoming tide, late afternoon, a couple of hours before sunset. Our afternoon Nemesis—howling wind—hadn't kept it's usual appointment and the waters of the "Middle Ground," that area of the bay between the Golden Gate Bridge, the Bay Bridge and just above the Richmond/San Rafael bridge, had remained placid all day—except for the expectant wakes of boats ranging from skiffs and party boats to high-speed ferries and tugs.

Conditions had allowed us to scour the water like a Brillo pad and we'd put 40 or more miles on my new Western Eagle Skiff. I was indeed glad Prime Time II was powered with Yamaha's new F100, four-stroke, an incredible powerhouse that consumed a third or more less fuel than my old two-stroke outboard would have. We had worked shallow flats, pebble beaches, sandy beaches, precipitous rocky points, current lines, pilings, rip-rap banks, islands, weed edges and even open water under working birds. We found a few nice striped bass willing to eat our flies just about everywhere but none topped six pounds—typical schoolies, but a serious hoot on 7- to 9-weight rods, nonetheless.

High tide, late afternoon—magic time upon us. I was hoping a few larger bass would be prowling a long bottom depression which ran 10 to 12 feet deep, paralleling a rocky shoreline a good distance, just north of the Richmond/San Rafael Bridge. I positioned my skiff so I could glide slowly with the tide and a gentle breeze, a long cast from the bank and making any needed adjustments with my electric motor. Conditions were perfect! Within minutes John tagged an eight-pounder on an SPS Flashtail (FT) Whistler. I was next with one around six pounds followed by another which bogied at eight— both duped by a chartreuse and white FT Whistler. We knew there had to be more stripers terrorizing bait in that depression so I repositioned the skiff at the top of the trough for another pass. About half way through the run I stuck a nice one on the second pull which bulldozed into about 40 yards of backing; and when John was just about ready to end his retrieve, a beaut slammed his Whistler at the rod tip. Doubles! We had the classical drill going for awhile—passing rods over and under to avoid crossed lines and we did whoop it up! What a way to end the day! Mine bogied at ten pounds and John's pushed 12 1/2 pounds. Not giants but good stripers on fly no matter where you find them.

For more than 35 years my San Francisco bay home turf has been South San Francisco Bay, that area from China Basin to the San Mateo bridge. It had been more than 25 years since I'd fished the Middle Ground. The summer and fall of 1998 and 1999 produced some spec-

tacular striped bass angling in this area, while south bay action had been extremely sporadic. At the urging of friends who had become intimate with the Middle Ground, experiencing superlative fly-rod action in recent years, I had decided to give it another try.

In August of 1999, San Francisco Bay vet, Bob Valentine graciously chauffeured me around the Middle Ground, showing me his approach to the area's superb

Top: John Ryzanich displays the "double" he and the author took on a productive afternoon fishing the Middle Ground.

Lower left: The author spent many of his early years on South San Francisco Bay seaching the productive pilings near the San Francisco airport.

striper fly-fishing. An excellent outing, I was shown new areas and we re-visited some with which I was familiar. I had forgotten how much prettier the Middle Ground scenery was along the Marin coastline, than that of south bay. I recalled what Russ Chatham, well-known author/artist and San Francisco Bay flyfishing pioneer, once said to me when we were discussing fly-fishing for bay stripers: "I know you're catching some big fish in south bay, Dan, but I just can't get behind the scenery down there."

A couple of weeks later, Captain Brian "Bud" Wilson, who guides fly-fishers and light-tackle enthusiasts into Middle Ground stripers, steered me around the

The author in his early 20s with a typical south bay bass (circa 1966). There were many more fish during the 50s, 60s, and 70s. Today most fish are released by fly-anglers.

Middle right: Captain Brian Wilson holds the author's rod while he photographs one of many "doubles" they had that productive day.

Far right: Productive islands: the Brothers.

same turf for another perspective of this productive region. We had an incredible day as well.

Working just a couple of beaches, points and tidal rips off one of the islands called Red Rock, I lost count after 50 bass using FT Clousers and FT Whistlers. Granted, most of the fish were schoolies, ranging from two to six pounds, but they smashed flies and both Captain Brian and I were beaming. I couldn't help but recall that outdoor writer Jules Cuenin had taken the first bay striper on fly from this same area in 1925. In just two Middle Ground refresher courses, provided by two very competent fly-anglers, I was ready to explore this productive area of San Francisco bay on my own again.

The Season

June marks the beginning of the migration of adult, post-spawners from the Sacramento/San Joaquin river/delta spawning grounds, down into San Francisco bay and adjacent ocean systems. However, fly-fishing in San Francisco Bay often begins as early as March with some very large fish that winter over in South San Francisco Bay instead of the delta region. This action can last through April. Once those storm the delta for spawning, schoolies take their place for what can be fast Spring action in many areas of the bay system, especially South Bay. Excellent fly-fishing for both schoolies and larger specimens commences in the Middle Ground as early as June but peaks during late summer and fall both in the bay and outside along traditional ocean beaches. This action often lasts until December. By late September, many fish are moving into the delta region, action building there, especially during October, November and December.

Productive Areas of the Middle Ground

While stripers can be taken from just about anywhere within the Bay's 450 miles of shoreline, in recent years the Middle Ground has had the right environmental conditions to draw both bait and bass together in large numbers. Feeding frenzies—"blitzes"—have become fairly common in this region and it pays to keep a vigilant eye open for whirling/diving birds and busting fish.

Some of the most productive areas of the Middle Ground, particularly in June when post spawners are returning from the rivers, are: Red Rock Island, and the Brothers and Sisters Islands. I can't tell you how many "Miss Piggies" have been hooked on fly off the Brothers

and Sisters in June, many of which can't be stopped from reaching nearby reefs, cutting even the heaviest tippets. Hooks are straightened, tippets snapped and even rods have been busted trying to stop these freight-train stripers.

Other productive areas include the grassy flats, rocky shorelines and piling structure ranging from north of Point Richmond on the east side, to as far south as the Emeryville flats at the Bay Bridge. One superb flats area is located just south of the Richmond harbor rock wall, including those flats and beaches around Brooks Island south to Fleming Point. On the east side of the Richmond San Rafael Bridge (RSB) and to the north, other good areas exist around Cypress Point, Castro Point, Point Molate and Point San Pablo.

One the west side, in San Rafael Bay, the Brick Yard

shoreline, north of the RSB, running west from Point San Pedro can be superb at times, spring, summer and fall. This is a traditional trolling area but fly-casters score well too. The Marin Islands can shine at times, as well as the open water just north of the RSB near channel marker 17. Look for bird activity here. The RSB pilings are known producers of bass of all sizes at both ends of the bridge, particularly during low light. This is where Russ Chatham took his world-record 34-pounder. Point San Quentin itself and its shoreline running west can also shine, and is a stable hot spot. Further south, the rock breakwater of the marina at Paradise Cay can

often be stellar, as well as the many sand and pebble beaches, rocky shorelines and points found along the entire Tiburon Peninsula from Paradise to Bluff Point and across Raccoon Straits to Angel Island. This entire region is loaded with striper dining rooms. Work pilings, rocks, rocky points with current seams, rip-rack banks, beaches and, above all, keep a vigilant eye peeled for working birds and busting fish, especially in the area of Southampton shoals.

Richardson's Bay is also part of the Middle Ground and it can be very fruitful for both boat anglers and wade-fishers. The most productive areas of Richardson's Bay are the points and beaches from Strawberry Point to the Highway 101 bridge on the east side of the bay. Just outside Richardson's Bay, toward the Golden Gate, the area from Yellow Bluff to Lime Point can be excellent at times.

The southwest end of Angel Island from Knox Point to Blunt Point, along the beaches can be superlative, wind permitting. Ditto for the east side of the island. There is also excellent habitat from Bluff Point to Point Tiburon on incoming tide. And finally, the rock walls, pilings, points and rocky shorelines around Treasure Island often attract schools feeding stripers.

Moon Phase and Productive Tides

Here are some general rules with regard to the best moon phases and tides for fly-fishing the San Francisco Bay system:

When chasing stripers with fly, the most consistently producing moon phases are the quarter moon phases which produce neap tides. Neap tides are the smaller tides with weaker currents and less water exchange between high and low tide. Neap tides keep the productive flats flooded as opposed to the huge spring tides that drain them dry; and, you will almost always have an early morning high. Fish are not in the deep, fast tidal rips during neap tides but are usually up on the flats in marauding pods, or schools, chasing bait around the above-mentioned structure.

During spring tides—full and new moon periods that produce larger tidal swings, stripers will be very scarce on the flats. Most will be in deep, fast water working on bait being swept along with the heavy flows. The early morning tide will almost always be a minus low which means no water (or fish) on the flats and when it comes back it's usually afternoon, and it's turbid from strong wind-chop. Fish the bay on neap tides which occur every other week. Good fly-fishing can be had from a day or two before to two or three days following the first day of the quarter moon. Most calendars indicate moon phases and it's very easy to plan your outings accordingly. You should also have a good, easy-to-read tide table for San Francisco Bay. Of course these are just guidelines and there are always exceptions. It's smart to keep a tidal/fishing log in order to learn which areas fish best on certain tides and moon phases.

Boats and Wade Fishing

If there's one thing I've learned about fly-fishing for bay and delta stripers—stripers anywhere for that matter—is that being mobile provides a huge advantage over those fishing afoot or in personal water devices such as float tubes and kick boats. Stripers are a peripatetic lot and are constantly on the move. The dinning room may be off a particular beach, flat or point one day or hour, and somewhere different the next. Accordingly, a boat provides the greatest advantage. You can fish from boats as small as 12- to 14 feet in length but because the bay's Nemesis—wind—comes up almost every afternoon, and sometimes very quickly, a larger boat ranging from 16 to 20 feet long provides the safest platform if you plan to test the smorgasbord beats on both sides of the Middle Ground. In addition to wind waves, you'll encounter wakes generated by tug boats and high-speed ferries, large enough to please even the most jaded surfer. However, boats shouldn't be so large or draw so much water they can't be easily maneuvered with an electric motor, or venture into three or four feet of water. Center-console styles, in either glass or aluminum, are perfect for bay waters.

This is not to say you can't fish some areas safely and with good success from a kick boat that can also be rowed, a pram or kayak. Doug Lovell, bay/delta guide and fly-shop owner, often fishes the bay from his kick boat as does his partner, Leo Siren. They often score big time from the pontoon boats in several areas of the

Above: Anglers working rocky points at the Brickyard.

Right: Shooting heads are the lines of choice for most bay vets, although some now use the "integrated heads" offered by Rio, Scientific Anglers and others.

Middle Ground: Berkley flats, Albany flats and the Richmond flats, near Point Richmond and around Brook's Island; and, in Richardson's Bay, just to name a few likely spots.

Wading is probably the most limiting but fly-rodding SF Bay stripers from the shore can be productive in certain areas. Finding the productive areas will take some hunting but if you see anglers tossing plugs and jigs from shorelines, rocky banks and points, you can bet you'll have opportunities there with a fly. I know of many who score big time at night or just before dawn from the flats mentioned above on very high tides and never wade deeper than their knees. Big fish will move onto shallow flats at night on big spring tides, flats they'll never venture onto during daylight hours. Remember: it's unlawful to fish the bay system from a boat at night but it's perfectly legal afoot. Wade safe, and always fish with a partner.

Tackling Up

If you have steelhead tackle, rods ranging from 8- to 10-weight and reels with a good drag and ample backing capacity, you've got striper tackle. In fact, you can even get by with a 7-weight rod if you know how to handle yourself properly with regard to slugfests. My favorite all-round package is 9-weight—light enough to enjoy the bantam weights but with enough testosterone to land Big Moe in open water.

Most bay vets use shooting-head systems to cover the column, including floaters for surface action with poppers and Gurglers. Heads which are connected to a coated shooting line of around .035 diameter or a mono-type shooting line such as Rio's clear intermediate in .030, work splendidly. Braided mono shooting line is also used by some, but it has a propensity to blow around and tangle more. For all-round use, I'd suggest one of the coated shooting lines such as Scientific Anglers Mastery saltwater floating shooting line in .035 diameter. Place a large, 50-pound braided mono loop on each end of the shooting line and also on the shooting head. These loops provide smooth, strong connections which permit quick

head changes to meet varied conditions. The most productive densities are type three to seven with Cortland's LC-13 lead core being the most popular for depths ranging deeper than seven feet or when working rips and strong currents. Intermediate sinkers can be productive in our bay waters but most have found that the fly that gets there first, wins. If you don't like shooting heads, instead preferring a similar casting line without the loop splice connection, there are "integrated shooting heads," as some have called them. Teeny, Rio, Airflo and Scientific Anglers all produce a sinking-head line that casts like a shooting head and gets down like an anvil sinks. My personal favorite is the Rio 350 Cold Water Striper line. Use sizes from 250 to 400 for best results. Most top guns use the traditional "countdown method" to determine the holding depth of the fish. Of course you can use a standard WF floating line for surface duty but I prefer a floating head for that, too.

Keep leaders simple: six to seven feet of your favorite soft, 20-pound mono (I like Berkley Big Game) is all you need for sinking lines. Tie a triple surgeon's loop in one end to the loop on the leader end of the line and use a good loop knot such as Lefty's non-slip mono loop to attach the fly. For floating lines, a simple tapered leader ten feet long is perfect.

Flies

Prevailing baitfishes in SF Bay include: anchovies, smelt, herring, shiner perch (and other perch species), gobies, bullheads and others. The most important are the anchovies, smelt and shiner perch. Accordingly your flies should suggest these species. That's not a difficult task, however, since we have long had the right flies available, proven patterns for more than 3 decades. In my experience, the top four fly-styles are: Flashtail Whistlers; Flashtail Clousers; Sar-Mul-Mac in anchovy, sardine and mackerel; and Lefty's Deceivers. Other good bets are Given's Barred 'N Black and various eel patterns. I've probably narrowed my selection for sinking flies to FT Whistlers, Clousers and Sar-Mul-Macs because these patterns cover all the bait species, have the right head-sinking, dipping and diving action and push lots of water—a desired trait since bay waters are slightly turbid, especially when the wind is up.

Best colors: white/red; white/griz; white/pink/purple (SPS: shad/perch simulator); black/griz; yellow/red; white/chartreuse and white/brown. If I only had one color for bay stripers it would be black/griz. All of my Whistlers and Clousers are now tied on 60-degree jig hooks which are absolutely superior when it comes to hooking and tracking correctly with hook point up. I'm currently using Eagle Claw's 413, 60-degree jig hook in sizes 2/0 through 4/0, with 3/0 being a good all-round

Top: *The productive breakwater of Paradise Marina.*

Left: *"Tease 'em to please 'em" is best done with a single-handed retrieve.*

average. Fly length should range from three to seven inches, with four to five inches, including flashtails, about right for most circumstances, especially in late summer or fall when bait is larger.

For topwater work, nothing beats a Gurgler or Crease fly. These are deadly!

Tease 'Em to Please 'Em

The double-handed retrieve is a favorite with many east coast striper devotees, but for bay/delta bass, a varied, single-handed pull is considerably better. Tease "em to please 'em is the right approach. This means get their attention with a series of two or three long, hard, fast pulls which pushes water and catches eyes, slow down with two or three slower pulls slightly shorter, then stop the fly and let it drop head first a moment, suggesting an injured bait. Pull it hard and fast again, stop-and-drop, fast slow, short, long—tease, tease, tease! You should stop-and-drop at least three times during your retrieve. Imagine a striper with its nose right on the tail of your fly. You're the salesman, it's interested but not convinced to buy. You've got to close the deal. A Woolly Bugger retrieve ain't gonna close the deal. If you're retrieving properly, by day's end, you'll have scored well but your elbow is going to hurt like hell.

Always retrieve the fly to within sight of your rod tip and then hover the fly right at the surface a few seconds before completing the rollcast pickup. It's amazing how many fish follow and will blast the fly right at the rod tip or off the surface. Conversely, always keep a tight line and rod tip pointed down and directly at the fly while it's sinking. I can't tell you how many stripers have eaten my fly on the sink. Hundreds!

Electronics

A good portable or dash-mounted depth/fish-finder that can side bottom scan simultaneously is a huge advantage. My favorite portable scanner is Bottom Line's Buddy 2200. Any high-end dash-mount will do.

As the lead narrative indicated, John Ryzanych and I had a splendid outing on the bay that day and I had many others well into late September when I pulled the plug and headed for the delta in October. Of course I could have continued to fish the Middle Ground with great expectations for another two months or more. Trust me when I say it won't be another 25 years before I hit the Middle Ground again. In fact, I'm looking forward to more Middle Ground action this coming summer and fall.

Summation

When: Peak period June through November

Where: San Francisco Bay between Golden Gate Bridge, Bay Bridge and the Sisters Islands north of the Richmond San Rafael Bridge.

Headquarters: Myriad motels and hotels in Richmond, San Rafael, Sausalito, San Francisco and Oakland

Appropriate gear: Rods 7- to 10-weight, sinking shooting heads from type 3 to type 7, including LC-13 lead core, with a coated shooting line around .035 in diameter. Mono-type shooting lines can also be employed. Floating shooting heads or full, WF floating lines are useful when poppers and Gurglers are working. Leaders for sinking lines shouldn't be longer than 7 feet and test from 15 to 20 pounds. Leaders for floating lines should test the same but be around 10 feet in length.

Useful fly patterns: Flashtail Whistlers; Flashtail Clousers; Sar-Mul-Mac; Lefty's Deceiver; and Given's Barred 'N Black work well for subsurface work. Standard poppers, sliders and foam Gurglers suffice for the top. Gurglers are especially productive.

Hot flies: Flashtail Whistlers; Flashtail Clousers and Sar-Mul-Macs.

Necessary accessories: Rain gear or wind breaker, warm clothes (someone once said the coldest winter day they ever experienced was a summer day on San Francisco Bay), sunglasses, hat, Peterson's Stripping Guards for your stripping finger, sunscreen and Sun Gloves for protecting your hands.

Licenses: California fishing license with striped-bass stamp or a two-day to ten-day nonresident fishing license with striped-bass stamp. Licenses available at fly-shops and marina tackle stores.

Guides: Fish First Guide Service, Doug Lovell and Leo Siren, PO Box 7215, Berkeley CA 94707, phone 510-526-1937; Prime Time Guide Service, Captain Dan Blanton, 14720 Amberwood Lane, Morgan Hill, CA 94037, phone 408-778-0602

Maps/charts: Fish-n-Map Co. available at most shops and marinas for around 6 dollars.

Where to stay: Various hotels in the San Francisco Bay Area.

CHAPTER 3

California Delta:
New Home Waters

The magic hour: low light and a time for fast action and big fish.

Inset: The author displays a schoolie taken at prime time on the delta—sunset on a hazy fall evening. Delta sunrises and sunsets are brilliant.

H ome water: most serious fly-anglers have staked out theirs and honor it with reverence. It's special above all others. When it came to the salt chuck, my home water was San Francisco Bay where I first started my saltwater fly-fishing career more than 45 years ago, catching striped bass, my favorite home-water species. In 1992 that changed. My favorite striper home water is now the California delta. Don't get me wrong, I still love chasing bay stripers during summer and early fall, but after spending the last 11 autumn and winter seasons feeding flies to delta stripers and largemouth bass, I've got a new home water, a new love. I now anxiously await October, the start of the delta striper season and dread it when it ends in May.

When the first Spanish explorers viewed the vast California delta from atop Mt. Diablo in spring of 1772, they thought they were looking at an immense lake. The delta's major rivers and tributaries had spilled their banks, flooding sprawling lowlands. During summer, flood waters receded, the area was home to native Indians and was rich in fish and wildlife, later becoming one of the most fertile farming regions in the world. It was also destined to become one of the finest striped-bass fisheries anywhere, with over 1,000 miles of navigable waterways—rivers and inter-connecting lakes and sloughs—drawing fly-anglers from near and far. Not only has our Backcountry, as I call it, become extremely popular with California fly-rodders, it's also become stellar with traveling anglers, world-wide, as a fishing or vacation destination. It's also a perfect angling opportunity for those in the Bay Area for business or visiting friends or relatives.

Venturing into the delta is like taking a step back decades in time. Within minutes of pushing off the dock, you'll find yourself surrounded by a vast wilderness comprised of watercourses containing vast numbers of both striped bass and largemouth bass during peak season. Wildlife abounds! You'll wonder just how all of it has miraculously sustained its unique beauty and country charm while only an hour from one of the most densely populated metropolitan sprawls in the country. And, it's future has been fairly secured by a massive ongoing delta conservation/restoration program, headed by CalFed and supported by dozens of other conservation and angling organizations.

A Little More History

By the end of California's Gold Rush era, the region became settled by mostly farmers and a few businessmen who recognized the vast potential of the fertile peat

soil bordering the river banks—bottom land that would have to be protected from raging winter floods.

Upon the completion of the Transcontinental railroad, a huge surplus of Chinese laborers became available to start building the levees needed to protect the

farmland. Later, huge clamshell dredges built the remaining levees that by 1930 had reclaimed some 700,000 acres of the richest farmland in the world, forming 55 man-made islands. Islands surrounded by sloughs, channels and deepened natural waterways—farming tracts protected from raging winter waters by rock and earthen levees.

It took awhile but the lack of jetty maintenance caused some of the levees to fail during years of extreme flooding, reclaiming some of the islands, turning them into shallow lakes surrounded by deep-water channels, sloughs or the rivers. Some were pumped dry again, others were left to

Lefty Kreh and Bob Clouser have fished the delta several times with the author. Here Lefty hefts a nice striper for Bob Clouser.

Left: House-boating the delta is another great way to explore this wonderland.

become prolific, shallow, weedy lakes. These are now some of the top producing striper and largemouth bass tidal waters in the country.

The Lakes

There are four of these lakes within the delta region that are of importance to the fly-angler: Franks Track, Sherman Island, Big Break and Mildred Island. When you look at a recent chart of thed delta, you'll quickly

extremely well when the fish are there.

Target areas: the islands, rock walls, depressions, cuts with current edges, points, and weed edges in seven to eight feet of water, especially near main current flows, with fairly deep, open water nearby. Of course channels and openings within weed beds can always produce both stripers and largemouth bass, as can all of the above. Oh, one other thing: duck hunters also use Franks Tract and station floating blinds in pre-assigned areas, usually near a weed-covered hump. The blinds attract threadfin shad (the predominant forage fish) and others, which in turn attract stripers. Many of us mark certain blinds on our GPS units but we never try to fish them if hunters are using them. This is good advice for obvious reasons.

A keen tactic is to first find a weed-free bottom, then locate a weed edge in seven to eight feet of water and run that edge using an electric motor, casting toward open

Above: When the levee walls broke during high water, flood waters turned farming islands into productive tidal lakes.

Middle: Wildlife abounds in the delta with a proliferation of shorebirds and water fowl.

Lower right: Rock-lined levee walls are productive areas, drop your fly as close as possible to the rocks or weed edges and use a fast, erratic retrieve, stalling the fly to let it fall at least twice during the retrieve. The author shows the results.

discover that Franks Tract is the hub of this vast network of waterways having approximately ten miles of shoreline, with a maximum depth of about 12 feet at high tide except for a couple of trenches that descend to around 25 feet.

Franks Track (often referred to as just the "Tract") is encircled by channels, called sloughs, some of which were actually original river tributaries. They average 25 feet in depth, but with areas of shallow, productive flats. The Tract itself is laced with tule banks, vast, weedy flats, bars, tule islands, depressions, humps, cuts and long, rock-lined levee walls—grocery stores for hungry bass.

The west side of Franks Tract is bordered by Bethel Island, the only island of the original 55 that has been developed into a small town, having all the amenities anglers need. Most all the rest have remained as undeveloped, private farm or state land. Once you leave the area of Bethel Island and venture out into the vastness of the delta, except to encounter few others, especially during mid-week.

Recent wet, warm, winters have promoted heavy weed growth in Franks Tract to the detriment of some angling opportunities. Just about the entire west and southwest portion of the lake is now nearly unfishable due to prolific weed growth (egeria densia). Many other areas of the lake are still fairly weed-free and produce

water. Conversely, positioning the boat a long cast from the weed edge and working it from open water produces too. A great way to locate these weed edges and channels is to reconnoiter during a minus low tide. Mark your chart or save them as a waypoint on your GPS.

One of the most consistent big-fish producers of the four delta lakes is Mildred Island, the deepest of the four lakes, because it hasn't been silted in. The average shoreline depth of Mildred is 10 to 12 feet, with some banks averaging 14 to 18 feet at high tide. A weed ribbon circumvents the entire lake, that ranges from just a few feet wide to more than a dozen. Generally, these weed edges are steep-sided, and your flies can be dropped within a foot or so of the edge without fear of fouling on salad. Both stripers and largemouth patrol this structure and use it to pin bait species against. It makes sense, then, to work the deeper banks and weed lines when targeting the larger stripers often stalking this structure.

Mildred also has three submerged orchards, all of

which are striper magnets. It's within the sub-surface limbs that baitfish take refuge, or try to at least, from marauding striped bass. It's always a good bet to search the woods with sinking lines and flies with double wire snag guards. Action can be staggering in these orchards at times. If you stick a Moe in the woods, hold on to your running line and pull like hell! Light tippets have no place when fishing wood! One of the best coves hosting the largest of the drowned orchards has been dubbed "Bay of Tears" for obvious reasons.

One of my largest delta stripers, a 32-pounder, came from the base of an old stump protruding from the water. I was fishing with my son Rich and Jose Silva both accomplished fly-anglers. It was a classic case of the "fly that gets there first wins." My big, chartreuse - and-white FT Clouser hit the water first and closest to the mossy stump. The Big Moe ate it almost instantly in a swirl of white water that looked like someone had flushed a 100-gallon toilet. The fish tore away, almost beaching itself. I put the electric motor into high reverse and pulled like a demon. Luck was with me and the big bass turned and ran toward deep water. The rest is history. That particular cove we were in has been called Big Fish Cove ever since.

Mildred also has her share of cuts (breaks) in her old levee walls and at

times the incoming tide, resulting in current edges and eddies forming off of the tule points in the breaks, can produce superb results. In contrast, the waters in her many deep coves along both the eastern and western shores, only rise and fall with the tides but still produce incredible results at times. It's mayhem when the bass corral shad in the apexes of these deeper coves. One of the best areas can be the north end of Mildred on either

side of the west orchard in water ranging from right against the weed edge to offshore in depths of 10 to 12 feet. Fan cast in deeper water, work the edges of the weed lines.

Always look for working birds and busting fish, particularly in the open areas of the lake and around the southwest orchard. I don't spend much effort on "jump-fishing," since often the fish are only sub-size schoolies, but occasionally the surface action can be a mother lode of hefty stripers and it's worth checking out. Ditto for all the other delta lakes when it comes to working birds.

Above: Captain Brian Wilson displays a good one taken from a weed edge.

Middle: A nice one from a weed edge.

Lower left: When the levee walls broke during high water, flood waters turned farming islands into productive tidal lakes. An old orchard, branches piercing the surface, becomes a striper hot-spot at times.

October/November is prime topwater action time, especially with a foam Gurgler—another eastern transplant. One season not long ago on Franks Tract I got into some heart-stopping Gurgler action along a weed edge that had double-digit fish pushing each other out of the way, competing for the 3/0 Gurgler. I landed a dozen or more big bass, missing as many more. The surface blow-ups were incredible! Hilarious fun!

Sherman Lake can be another scorcher and is bordered on one side by the Sacramento River and on the other by the San Joaquin. The cuts on the Sacramento side, in water ranging from four to eight feet deep, often produce outstanding catches of larger fish. Work the current seams on incoming water. Another good area is the southwest end, again around breaks and in weed bed channels. Ditto for some of its meandering sloughs and creeks, especially where they form wide corners and coves.

Big Break is the fourth productive lake, and while very shallow from siltation, the breaks, channels, holes and islands can still produce stellar catches of stripers and black bass. Boat ramps are available on all the lakes except Mildred.

Rivers and Sloughs

Delta lakes, rivers and sloughs can produce any time during the course of the season but mid-winter, from December on, is when the rivers and sloughs shine. The San Joaquin, both forks of the Mokelumne, False River, Connection slough, Fisherman's Cut, Sandmound slough, Potato slough, Latham slough and Middle River (just to name a few), can all produce splendidly with some quality fish. Look for flats that rise from 25 or 30 feet of water to that ranging from 8 to 15 feet. Stripers love flats and this is where you'll often find them. Target down-current points of tule islands, casting tight to the point and working the slope. Cast to the weed edges that form along the levee rock walls, especially walls that have ledges and flats. It often pays to get in close and then make presentations that parallel the weed edges, keeping the fly in the "Meat Bucket" longer. This tack is especially good if you are not a strong caster. Side sloughs that offer some deep water and protection from wind can be honey holes. Pumps that are actively pumping water from islands back into a slough can be scorching at times, as are cuts in levees that drain lakes back into a river or slough.

There is one such place I call the Junk Yard and often when the tide is ebbing and water is flowing out of a shallow lake forming a nice current seam, stripers line up to

Top right: Mildred Lake has three drowned orchards which are very productive at times.

Middle: One of the author's largest stripers came from the base of an old stump protruding from the water.

Lower: Rocky levee walls with weed beds and tules are high-percentage spots.

ambush bait being flushed out with the tide. They lay so close to the bank, in less than two feet of water and under overhanging blackberry bushes, that getting a cast in close enough is difficult. The last time I fished this spot the fishing Gods blessed me. The sun was setting behind Mt. Diablo and the sky way resplendent in a wash of gold and violet. To the east, in the direction I was casting, the water and bank was bathed in a soft, golden light while a full moon was rising simultaneously as the sun set. The air was still and Canada geese were dropping in for an evening meal. A family of river otters crossed the slough 100 feet below me making their way into the tules and blackberry vines lining the levee wall. Life just couldn't be better—or could it?

My first cast produced a splendid fish that took the

fly less than two feet from the bank, sending water and weeds skyward in a frightening boil. The fish ran for the depths of the slough and after a long run and a short, deep-down slugfest, I was able to latch the jaws of my Boga Grip to a fat 25-pounder. For the next hour and a half, well after sunset and under brilliant moonlight, fish after fish took my fly, many of them teeners. I was all alone except for the bass, the geese, the otters and the fishing Gods. What a way to end the day. It couldn't have been better.

Covering the Water

Being able to scour a lot of water during the course of a day is important. Striper schools are extremely itinerate (at peak season there can be a few fish caught at just about every good spot) and to experience fast action or to find that dream school of aggressive teeners, keep moving. Never homestead a spot! If you've pounded the water thoroughly for 15 or 20 minutes without reward, move! Keep moving until you find fish. The more good areas you know, the greater your chances will be of finding

Above: Calm flat water seems to produce the fastest fishing throughout the delta. Here Pete Valconesi puts the final touches on a big fish.

Left: Getting in close and casting parallel works great.

fast action. Try to discover a new spot every time you venture out. One of the best ways I know to learn the delta is to rent a house boat from one of many marinas and spend a week's vacation on the delta using the houseboat as your personal floating lodge. I did this for three seasons in a row, shortening my learning curve hugely. Keep a journal of places, times, tides and productivity. Doing so will help narrow the playing field. And, above all—if it looks fishy, try it! More than once!

Reasonable Expectations

The delta has a reputation for rewarding its top anglers with big-number days—fish to hand often exceeding 30 or more, with many double-digit fish in the mix. However, reasonable expectations, considering average conditions and average angler knowledge/skill, even when being guided, should be around 10 to 15 fish a day. Count your blessing when the tally rises higher.

Conditions

Weather: It's everything! Good weather, calm, no-wind conditions. The flatter the better! Often in between winter storms, delta waters become glass. This is when fly-fishing sparkles. Dense tule fog (ground radiated fog), which frequently tents the delta, particularly after a storm, can be both bane and boon. Bane: you can't see where you're going and you'll have to navigate via compass or GPS and you'll have to be damned careful of other boaters. Boon: no wind, which lets you cover the water like a tent. Good electronics plus a VHS radio or cell phone are tremendous aids to delta boaters. It's also a good idea to have a membership in one of the towing services, such as Vessel Assist, the AAA of the waterways.

Tides and Moon Phases

While you can enjoy fast action during the quarter-moon phase and resulting neap tides, when it comes to the lakes, the best action occurs during the full and new moon (spring tides). Delta stripers are extremely current orientated, usually going off the bite during slack tide. Full or new moon phases produce big movements of water in the delta: an early morning high shortly before or after sunrise, followed by falling water until around noon when the tide goes slack—a perfect time for having lunch at the Sugar Barge restaurant, or to head for the houseboat for lunch and a siesta if you happen to be on a houseboating vacation, a marvelous yet inexpensive way to learn and enjoy the delta. You'll have incoming water all afternoon, with maximum flood just before, to just after dark. Fishing many of the cuts on falling water a few hours after sunset can produce extraordinary fly rod catches. The sloughs seem to fish best on the neap tides, particularly during winter when there is more water in the delta system. The lesser current produced by neap tides makes fishing the rivers and sloughs easier and seems to muddy the water less. Falling water often produces best in the sloughs but this is not etched in granite. Of course this is not to say you won't enjoy good success during either neap or spring tide phases. Go whenever you can!

Tackling Up

Tackling up for delta stripers and black bass doesn't require high-end equipment, but your gear should be on a par with good steelhead or salmon equipment. You can use anything from a 7-weight stick to an 11-weight but I'm convinced the best all-round rod-weight is a nine, up-lined by at least two line sizes when using shooting heads. Sage, T&T, Loomis, Winston, Redington, Saint Croix and others of similar stature are all good choices.

The most popular line-type is a 30-foot shooting

Right: Author with a 30-pounder taken from a slough in winter.

Far right: Dense tule fog can move in at any time or be there at dawn; some days it's not too thick but never venture onto the delta without a GPS unit or at least a compass.

head looped to a mono-type shooting or a good coated shooting line such as SA's Mastery floating saltwater shooting line in .035 diameter or Rio's clear intermediate mono shooting line in .030 diameter. I rig at least two rods, one with a type 4 to 7 sinking density and another with a 30-foot lead-core shooting head of Cortland's LC-13. Another favorite line of mine is what I call the 20/10 lead tip. It's made from an 11-weight, type -4 shooting head. The first ten feet are cut off the front taper and are replaced with ten feet of LC-13 lead-core, via inter-connecting 50-pound braided mono loops. The standard type-4 sinking head is used when plying water six feet and shallower, the 20/10 line targets depths of eight to ten feet and the lead-core head lets you scratch bottom easily in waters ranging from ten to 20 feet, with stiff currents. Other great choices if you don't like shooting heads are: Rio's Cold Water Striper line in 250 to 350 grains; Airflo's DF 400 and similar types produced by Scientific Anglers and Cortland. Efficiency is the hallmark of success with no wasted time-in-motion! Use the fastest sinking line the best producing retrieve will permit—unless, of course, you're using poppers. For poppers I prefer a floating shooting head—size 11 for the 9-weight. Of course you can use a full length, WF floater, too.

Leaders: keep them simple! Use a six- to 9-foot length of high-quality 20-pound mono such as Berkley Big Game for a glass leader. Tie a surgeon's loop at one end for looping to the shooting head and use a good loop knot, such as the Kreh "non-slip mono loop" to tie on the fly. It couldn't be easier or more effective. Some anglers like to attach a bite leader of 30- or 40-pound mono to the class tippet. I don't find one necessary.

Large-arbor reels with a good drag are great but not necessary. Good choices include: Tibor Everglades; Islander, Loomis Syncrotech, and Redington Breakwater, ranging in size from 8 to 11. Of course you can get by with lesser-quality reels, and I particularly enjoy using Redington's GD reel in the 9/10 size. Regardless of which reel you choose be sure of solid drags and at least 150 yards of backing capacity.

Flies

There are countless fly patterns or styles that will score big time on backcountry stripers and largemouth bass but if I were to narrow it down to time-tested favorites, the list would include: Blanton's Flashtail Whistlers in sizes 3/0 and 4/0 and in SPS (shad/perch simulator); red/white/griz; red/yellow/griz; white/chartreuse, and black/griz; Blanton's Sar-Mul-Mac in the same sizes and in the sardine, anchovy or mackerel pattern; Flashtail Clousers ranging in size from 2/0 to 4/0 in the same colors as the Whistlers; Lefty's Deceivers; Half & Halfs; and Trey Combs' Sea Habits, same colors and sizes; various poppers including Bob Bangers' Murakoshi poppers and a huge favorite with many of us, the Gartside Foam Gurgler in size 2/0 to 3/0.

The Season

Fall and winter are prime time in the delta. Summer? In summer the water warms into the high 70s and 80s and the majority of the stripers have migrated down into the cooler bay/ocean system. The wind also howls incessantly during summer. Forget the delta from June through August, except on rare occasions.

The Sacramento/San Joaquin Delta offers the serious fly-rodder,one of the greatest angling experiences available today. It has become a favorite angling destination for those visiting the greater San Francisco Bay Area with many licensed guides to show them where and how

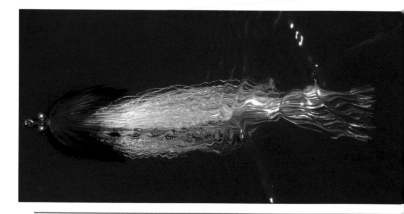

A Whistler is designed to push water, creating a water wave or wake the fish can feel and find.

it's done. This vast wildlife refuge harbors not only striped bass and largemouth bass but a gaggle of other splendid gamefish, too. It's also home to myriad species of shore birds and water fowl—egrets, sandhill cranes, great blue heron, bittern, geese, ducks, swans and many others. Foxes, beaver, otter, muskrats, raccoons, weasels, and other critters live there as well.

Like I said, it's now my home water, too!

Planning A Trip

Marinas/RV Parks/Restaurants

I consider the Sugar Barge Marina and RV Park located on Bethel Island as my home marina. The folks at the Sugar Barge have bent over backwards to accommodate fly-anglers. The launch ramp is open at all times. The RV park is five star with all the needed amenities. Restrooms are spotless as is the park. And, the Sugar Barge Restaurant is one of the finest in the Bay Area, rivaling any in San Francisco. The restaurant is open for dinner Wednesday through Sunday. The ambiance is incredible on full-moon nights. Contact number: (925) 684-8585. Address: 4515 Willow Road, Bethel Island, CA 94511.

There is also a launch ramp, fully rigged rental bass boats, camping and rental cabins at Lundborge Landing just down Piper slough from the Sugar Barge and reached via Gateway Road. The Landing Bar and Grill is open 24/7 for breakfast, lunch and dinner. Lunches are superb from a huge menu.

Russo's marina and campground is extremely popular with fly-fishers and is highly recommended. The Russo boys treat us right and Chuck Grandon, proprietor of Chuck's Bait & Tackle, located right on the docks at Russo's Marina, is the man to call for current information. Chuck has stocked his shop with all the right stuff: Custom-tied FlashTail Whistlers, Flashtail Clousers and Sar-Mul-Macs tied by Jay Murakoshi; rods, reels, shooting heads and shooting line—the works. He has ice, cold drinks, beer and wine, hot coffee and rolls when he opens at six a.m.; maps, tide schedules and just about anything else a visiting angler might need—including current information on water, weather and fishing conditions. Chuck can also connect you with a guide. He has completely outfitted four aluminum rental skiffs, set up for fly anglers. Give Chuck a call any time for current information. Closed Tuesdays. Phone: (925) 684-0668; PO Box 720, Bethel Island, CA 94511

The Rusty Porthole Restaurant/cocktail lounge, located just a short walk from Russo's campground, right on the levee at Boyd's Harbor, is absolutely great! The food is excellent, and you can't beat the waterfront ambiance. They serve breakfast, lunch and dinner. Many folks boat to the Rusty Porthole; I often come in for lunch, tying up at the dock when the tide goes slack around noon. You can't beat their Italian sausage sandwich! Closed Wednesdays. Of course, there are many other launch ramps and facilities located throughout the delta, but these are my favorites.

Licenses/Guides/General Information

Licenses: California fishing license with striped-bass stamp or a two-day to ten-day nonresident fishing license with striped-bass stamp. Licenses available at fly shops and marina tackle stores.

Guides: Fish First Guide Service, Doug Lovell and Leo Siren, PO Box 7215, Berkeley, CA 94707, phone 510-526-1937; Pacific Adventures Outfitters, Mike Costello, 445 Discovery Bay Blvd., Discovery Bay CA, 94514, 925-634-1280; Prime Time Guide Service, Captain Dan Blanton, 14720 Amberwood Lane, Morgan Hill, CA 94037, phone 408-778-0602

Necessary Accessories: Rain gear or wind breaker, warm clothes, sunglasses, hat, Peterson's Stripping Guards for your stripping finger, sunscreen and Sun Gloves for protecting your hands.

Maps/Charts: Fish-n-Map Co. available at most shops and marinas for around 6 dollars.

Houseboat Rentals

Vacationing on the delta using a rental houseboat (or your own if you have one) is a wonderful way to experience and learn the delta backcountry. During the off season, which usually starts soon after Labor Day, the weekly houseboat rental rates usually drop considerably with an off-season discount. Here are some of the top houseboat/fishing boat rental services. Call for rates and general information.

1. Herman & Helen's Marina
   Stockton, CA 800-676-4841
2. Delta Houseboat Rentals
   Stockton, CA 800-255-5561
3. Paradise Point Marina
   Stockton, CA 800-752-9669

CHAPTER 4

Largemouth Bass Wonderland

The California delta hosts more black-bass tournaments than any other place on earth.
Inset: The California delta is a largemouth bass wonderland. Angler Captain Brian Wilson with a nice bass.

Are you one of the many who have joined the growing ranks of warmwater fly-anglers? If not you ought to consider signing up. Indeed, interest in fly-fishing for a huge variety of warmwater species has profoundly increased during the past few decades. Fly-fishers are throwing flies at bass, pike, muskie, panfish, landlocked stripers, white bass and a hoard of others like never before, not only across this continent but abroad as well; and, they're having a great time doing it.

The most popular and accessible warmwater species in this country is the largemouth bass (LMB). It is rated as the most targeted sweet water species by gear anglers. Just ask the Bass Masters society. It's one of my favorite flygrabbers too.

I started my flyfishing career long ago pursuing bass and panfish in the local lakes and farm ponds close to my home in California's Santa Clara valley. My first fish on a fly was a bluegill, a monster as I recall. In retrospect, though, they all were monsters to me back then.

During a lifetime of warmwater fly-fishing following that event, I've taken my share of good-sized LMB on a variety of flies, poppers and hair bugs. Admittedly, though, only a few of those topped five or six pounds, with the vast majority averaging under three. Unless you had access to private lakes and ponds, lived in the Deep South or traveled afar, shots at lots of Big Moe bass on fly were scarce or in water too deep to be practical targets for northwestern fly-anglers.

For me, that all changed when I re-discovered the California delta, a LMB wonderland consisting of more than 1,000 miles of navigable water ways—rivers, sloughs and tidal lakes teeming with big bass. In fact, the delta is one of the most popular areas for black-bass tournaments and more of these competitions are held there than at any other place on earth. Recently, the 5-fish weight limit record for a national bass tournament weigh-in was shattered during a delta event. I don't recall the poundage but it was staggering. Delta bucketmouths of over 20 pounds have come to hand by conventional anglers and just this past season a 14-pounder and a 12-pounder where taken from delta waters by fly-anglers Doug Lovell and Kevin Doran. Doug's teener was taken on a chartreuse/white Flashtail Whistler and Kevin's fell for one of his own streamer creations.

Many believe the average size of our delta LMB has increased dramatically since of the introduction of a Florida strain of LMB and its subsequent hybridization with our northern strain. Makes sense; but all I know for sure is that ever since I started fly-fishing the delta again in 1992, I've lost count of the LMB over six pounds I've taken on fly, with many ranging better than

eight pounds. Three- and four-pounders are common. I'm still looking for my first 10-pounder on fly but I'm confident it won't be long in coming.

Above: Dave Whitlock lands a big delta largemouth bass.

Lower left: The author began his flyfishing career at age 11. His first fly-rod fish was a hefty bluegill.

Where to Start—Venturing Out

The total area of the California delta is massive and can be very intimidating to those not familiar with its lakes and meandering water courses. Where to begin? Well, if you were to take a chart of the delta and use it to play "Pin the Fly on the Bass," just about anywhere pinned would have some LMB in close proximity. They are just about everywhere, including a few smallmouth bass higher in the system. There's Franks Tract, Mildred Island, Sherman Lake, Big Break and literally dozens of sloughs, cuts and channels ranging all the way from Pittsburg to Stockton, not to mention rivers like the

Largemouth Bass Wonderland

float-tubers and kick-boaters can operate but I wouldn't personally recommended their use on most waterways for a variety of safety concerns: strong currents, huge boat wakes, snags, floating debris, dense tule fog and lots of very fast boats which may not see a tuber... The list goes on. Noting certain exceptions, delta water is just not a safe place for this form of personal watercraft.

In addition to great flyfishing potential, the Tract offers the fly-angler other amenities: good launching facilities, camping, dining and boat rentals. There is even flyfishing guide services for both stripers and black bass; and the area is only an hour-and-a-half or less drive from the greater San Francisco Bay Area.

Franks Tract and its adjoining sloughs, such as Piper, Sandmound, Connection, False River (aka Washington Cut), and nearby Fisherman's Cut, are all excellent places to find lots of LMB. But what about other productive regions?

There are other flooded islands which have long been productive LMB lakes. Again, these include: Mildred Island, Sherman Island and Big Break. Sherman and Big Break have launching ramps but Mildred doesn't. However, Mildred is close to several launch sites, including Russo's Marina and the Sugar Barge Marina on Bethel Island, and there's Holland Riverside Marina

Above: The author has lost count of the bass over four pounds he's taken on fly from the delta.

Lower right: Working flies on Frank's Tract, one of the best delta lakes for largemouth bass.

Sacramento, San Joaquin, Stanislaus, and both forks of the Mokelume. The enormity of it all can become mind-boggling.

A great place to start from is Franks Tract, which is often called the "Lake of the Delta." Franks Tract, the largest delta lake and located on the east side of Bethel Island, is the hub of this vast system of waterways. From there it's possible to range out to dozens of other productive areas.

Days could be spent tossing flies to LMB from a sea-worthy skiff equipped with an electric motor on Franks Tract, Little Franks Tract and in the myriad connecting sloughs, cuts and channels without venturing farther and you'd be happy as a hawg bass with a gut full of shad.

There are some areas within the delta system where

on Holland tract at the end of Delta Road. There are others in the Stockton area, checking a good delta chart will lead you to them.

Big Break is bordered by the San Joaquin river while Sherman Island is skirted by both the San Joaquin and the Sacramento rivers. There are miles of bass-filled sloughs and channels cris-crossing between all of these lakes ranging from Bethel Island to Stockton, back to Pittsburg and up the Sacramento to points past Courtland. Some of the best include: Sycamore, Whites, Little Potato, Whiskey, Disappointment, Latham and Old River, just to name a few more. Once you check out a chart, your eyes will bulge at the amount of bass-laden water within delta boundaries.

Bass Dining Rooms

The most productive structure holding delta blacks include: tule-covered berm points near cuts; rock-lined levee walls with weed beds and tule clumps; the new sea wall at Franks Tract; tree stumps; deadfall; willow and berry vine-lined banks; moss mats; irrigation pipes; tule banks near weed beds; weed edges almost anywhere, especially near cuts and current seams and old docks and pilings. All of these areas hold LMB at one time or another, some of which produce better during peak current flow, particularly on the ebb, which draws the bait and bass out of dense cover.

Take tule points for example: delta bass are extremely current orientated and take advantage of strong tidal flows which sweep helpless baitfish to them. Accordingly, black bass often stage near a tule point where strong currents flow through a cut. Hugging the tules and facing the current they ambush baitfish being swept into the cut. Cast your flies up-current, close to the tule bank and swim them down stream into the maws of waiting bass. Want to know which tule points and cuts are best? Just keep an eye on the tournament pros and mark the tule points and banks they fish on your chart. It won't take long to learn all of their secret spots...

Rock walls with weed lines, overhanging willows, deadfall and tules are also great producers of big bass, that feed there on a variety of things from minnows to crayfish. Position the boat a good cast away and drop the fly as close to the rocks or weed edges as possible, letting the fly sink for a four or five count while maintaining a tight line (bass often nail the fly on the sink). Retrieve the fly five or six feet and if a strike isn't forthcoming, let it sink a few seconds and then pull it slowly back to the boat or let it swim with the current. Poppers need only be worked a few feet before being cast back to shoreline structure again. Use your electric motor to move the boat slowly with the tidal flow, searching the length of the wall or to hold your position if concentrations of fish are encountered. A drag chain helps if current or wind push the boat too quickly.

Both LMB and stripers feed along rock walls. Some good areas include the east rock wall of Franks Tract, Sandmound Slough levee rocks and the entire rock-lined

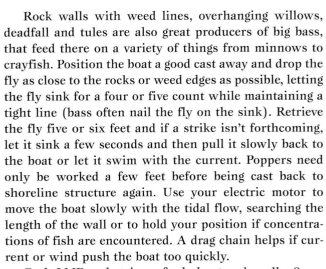

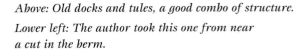

Above: Old docks and tules, a good combo of structure.
Lower left: The author took this one from near a cut in the berm.

perimeter of Quimby Island, just to name a few in the Franks Tract region. Concentrate on areas where currents flowing through a cut impact against the rock wall, where there are depressions or small coves in the wall or where cover such as cane, over-hanging brush and wild blackberries are growing. Always cast around tree stumps, pilings and deadfall. Irrigation pipes actively pumping water back into the sloughs are always good bets for both blacks and stripers.

Little Franks Tract, bordering the northwest end of Franks Tract, is loaded with submerged trees, old stumps, grass beds, rock walls and several productive breaks in the old levee walls. Some of my biggest largemouth bass have come from there. However, this lake has become extremely weedy and boating can be difficult, if not impossible, at low tide. Mildred Lake has lots of productive shoreline plus three flooded orchards that

ping explosions—ravenous bass crashing through the ceiling of the mat in an effort to engulf the hapless creature scurrying for its life. The best mats are those that are not too solid, having a "cottage cheese" consistency instead of those more like a thin carpet. Fly-anglers can get into this action, too, by using heavy flies armed with wire or heavy mono snag guards. Splat the fly onto the mat and then crawl it along at a medium pace—not too fast or slow. Hang on and make sure your pacemaker is working properly...

Kevin Doran (aka KD) is a long-time delta LMB fly vet. He has developed a spun deer-hair fly with a hard belly coating that adds weight and causes the hook to ride up for mat fishing. It's dubbed the KDM Rat. He has experienced excellent results mat fishing with this

Above: Ed Marcillac with a nice bass taken from structure near a break in the berm. Look for bass on current seams and near deadfall.

Right: Old deadfall, weed beds and tules, all the best big-bass structure.

can hold bass. Both Sherman Lake and Big Break offer all of the above structure and are loaded with LMB.

During the fall months when threadfin shad gang up for spawning, large grass beds located some distance from tule berms can be dynamite areas for schooling largemouth bass, particularly those beds located near cuts or tule berm points. Fast action can be had when the bass gang up in these weed beds and almost any good shad-imitating fly will score. Always keep a vigilant eye peeled for working birds and busting fish in the open areas of the lake where both largemouth bass and stripers collectively terrorize schools of shad.

Working the Mats and Pocket Structure

During high summer, moss mats form in shallow water around tule berms and levees. These mats provide shade and cover for LMB. Gear anglers have always loved to toss large, weedless plugs called Rats on top of the mats, crawling and hopping them along, leaving a sort of wake in the mat. This undulating trail brings on heartstop-

fly but is still testing it. I asked KD about his approach to successful fly-fishing for delta LMB. Here's what he offers:

"I target LMB from mid to late March through October. The LMB fishing is excellent all fall and winter but I forsake black bass for the striped ones. Focus on broken up tule berms and islands, open water next to riprap, pockets in tules, overhanging brush and trees, docks, weedy flats large and small, deadfall, peat berms and anything else bassy looking. Work tight to structure employing sidearm or underhand casts for the majority of presentations. Pinpoint casting is a big part of the game to be consistent, much more so than just casting to general areas. Work the tule pockets and every nook and cranny! You'll experience wonderful action using surface flies such as deer-hair sliders, divers, balsa poppers and Gurglers, but don't forget subsurface patterns as well, including V-worms, all with snag guards."

The Season

Now that you know where to go, what about when? Actually, you can take delta largemouth on flies year-round, with certain months producing better than others, with weather (wind) sometimes being a major factor.

As KD has said, spring is an excellent time to chase delta LMB. During March, April and early May, fly-fishing for blacks can be excellent just before and during the spawning period. Most of the fish will be on or close to the nest, however, since the delta has more water in it during this time than at any other, bass will be farther back into the cover during high tide, making it more difficult to reach them with flies. As KD noted, you need to pick pockets and accurate, tight-quarter presentations are a must. It is often best to target these areas at low

Above: The author with a nice bass taken from a rock-lined levee wall.

Left: Weed beds.

tide since the bass won't be as far back in the bush then, making them more accessible. Bait species will also be drawn from high tide-flooded structure to more open water, near edges.

Another important factor which is actually a deterrent to spring fishing is the incessant wind. It always seems to be blowing making it much more difficult to fly-fish, although it can still be done since there are many protected areas, particularly in the sloughs and backwaters/coves. And, the water can be very turbid caused by local run-off and large releases from dams on the various delta rivers. You need to pick your days during spring and also fish early and late in the day when winds are gentler.

Late-summer, fall and winter fly-fishing offer better conditions: water levels are not as high and turbid, the winds are generally nil, and these current-orientated LMB are keying on threadfin shad, the predominate forage fish, which means they'll be extremely aggressive, moving farther to intercept a well-designed fly or popper. September, October and November are my absolute favorite months; but December and January can produce very well, depending upon weather. What about high summer?

The delta is a multiple-use recreational area the entire year: fishermen, water-foul hunters and water

sports devotees all use it. High summer (late June, July and August) is the prime period for the latter, which are a Nemesis to black-bass anglers because they like to terrorize the same water we frequent. Though immense, the delta hasn't an appetite large enough to swallow the hordes of water-skiers, wake-boarders and jet-skiers that swarm to the region when temperatures sore into the 80s; and, you guessed it, the damned wind still blows then. Still, good bass'n can be had during torrid delta days. As in spring, fish early and late, confining yourself to areas that receive lesser boating traffic. You can fish during the week? Great!

What They Eat

Delta black-bass fodder includes such things as: threadfin shad; American shad; carp minnows; squaw fish; Sacramento black fish; smelt; a variety of panfish, lamprey eels and crawfish, among others. Accordingly, you'll need a variety of flies to cover the bases. There are lots of good ones from wihch to choose.

The predominate forage fish during prime time, however, is the threadfin shad, and you'd be hard pressed to come up with a better-producing moniker than my Flashtail Whistler—delta blacks just love them! Other top-notch patterns include: Blanton's Sar-Mul-Mac, 3/0, sardine and anchovy pattern; Flashtail JH (jig hook)

Clouser Minnow in various colors and sizes ranging from 1/0 to 3/0; Lefty's Deceivers, 1/0 to 3/0, various colors; Blanton's Bay-Delta Eelet, 3/0; Whitlock's Eel Worm, 2 to 2/0; Whitlock's hair jigs 2 to 2/0, various colors and Whitlock's Sheep Shad, 2 to 2/0, just to name a few of the best. All of these patterns can be fished without a weed guard, but for obvious reasons, it's best if they have one.

Again, poppers, sliders, Gurglers, hair bugs and Dahlberg Divers in a variety of sizes and colors can be productive, too, and should have a place in your arsenal of delta bass flies. Try surface flies on calm days when the water is oil-slick, early and late—bass bug time! Try manipulating Dahlberg Divers on a short leader attached to a type-four or faster, sinking head or a Rio DC Coldwater Striper line in 250 or 350. Let the head

Below: Because the bass are big, the general fly is large so there is a good chance of hooking into a big striper; rods with matching reels, ranging from 7- to 10-weight, are suggested.

Right: Big delta bass eat lots of things and they like large flies. The author's FT Whistler pattern is one of the best big-bass producers.

Far right: During high summer, you'll need to "pick the pockets" in the tules and wood structure.

sink to the bottom, pulling the fly below the surface. Retrieve the diver (or hair-head streamer) in a series of short to long pulls, pausing frequently to allow the buoyant fly to rise head-first toward the surface. This tactic is deadly! And, don't forget to rat the mats!

Tackling Up

You may be thinking that the sizes of the suggested flies are pretty damned big for LMB. Most fly-anglers use much smaller patterns which include a variety of small streamers and bucktails, including Buggers and the likes. Hey, they'll work too and you can use lighter rods, say 5- to 6-weight sticks, to deliver them. However, note again the predominant baitfish. They're big! Delta LMB eat big bait and it's the same bait stripers eat. The delta will be full of stripers during fall, winter and spring, and there are always a few there year round. It's common for LMB fly-fishers to hook many stripers as incidental catches, and vice versa for striper devotees who stick many LMB by accident. They eat the same things and frequent many of the same areas. Accordingly, 7- to 9-weight rods matched with a quality reel featuring a good drag and loaded with ample backing is heartily suggested. My favorite sticks are rated fast-action and while I do use lighter rods, a 9-weight is my work horse.

You'll need both sinking and floating lines. Up-lining at least one size with standard WF floating or intermediate tapers and two with shooting heads is recommended. Leaders needn't be too complicated and no

longer than around 9 feet in length, testing heavy. Twenty-pound tippets are advisable in order to rip big fish out of structure—another reason for beefier rods.

Finally, whenever plying a vast tidal area such as our California delta, being observant, keeping an open mind, having a willingness to break from convention and keeping good records are all vital to consistent success. If successful, pay attention to the details: location, time of day, moon phase and tidal stage. Keep a journal. Chances are great that when conditions repeat so will the frantic action.

The California delta is a miracle of nature remaining as one of the most productive wildlife areas on the continent, one teeming with both largemouth bass and striped bass and an endless variety birds and other wildlife—an area frozen in time, despite being surrounded by one of this country's most populated urban sprawls. If you like catching big largemouth bass on fly or want to give them a try, you'd be hard pressed to find a more productive or beautiful environment than the California delta.

Planning A Trip

When: Just about year-round with peak seasons in March/April/May/June and September through December. High summer can also be productive early morning and evening. Fishing is best when winds are calm and the tide is moving. Slack water is a good time for a break or lunch.

Where: The California delta's more than 1,000 miles of navigable water-ways: lakes, rivers and sloughs ranging from Antioch to Stockton with Franks Tract being the hub from which to radiate out into the backcountry. This vast area is only an hour to an hour-and-a-half from the greater San Francisco Bay/San Jose/Sacramento areas.

Headquarters: Brentwood and Bethel Island where you'll find motels, campgrounds, restaurants, marinas and campgrounds. Suggested motel in Brentwood is the Holiday Express Inn, phone: 1-925-634-6400; the best campground RV park on Bethel Island is the Sugar Barge RV park which has all the amenities, including a marina, launch ramp and 5-star restaurant, phone: 1-800-779-4100; another favored campground and marina is Russo's Marina on Bethel Island where you can also get current information, flies, fuel, drinks, licenses and even rent a boat from Chuck's Bait & Tackle on the docks at Russo's, phone: 1-925-684-0668.

Appropriate gear: 8 1/2- to 9-foot fly-rods ranging in weight from 7 to 9, WF floating and sinktip fly lines including sinking shooting heads in density 2 to 4, up-lined from one to two weights, with Rio's DS 26 or DC 26, bluewater or coldwater striper line in weight 300 or 350 being an excellent choice as a sinking line for presenting large, bulk flies. Leaders should range to 9 feet in length and test 15 to 20 pound. Reels should have a good drag and ample backing.

Useful fly patterns: Blanton's Flashtail Whistlers, Flashtail Clousers, Sar-Mul-Macs, Sea Habits, Lefty's Deceivers, V-worms, Rabbit Strip Leeches, Whitlock's Eel Worm, Whitlock's Sheep Shad, larger Woolly Buggers, balsa poppers, sliders, hair bugs, Tullis Wiggle Bugs and Gurglers, all with snag guards.

Necessary accessories: Hat, sunglasses, sunscreen, insect repellent, rain jacket (warm clothes in layers during winter), Sun Gloves, Peterson's Stripping Guards, stripping basket or similar fly-line management vessel such as Pro-Trim's Fly Line Tamer.

Licenses: A yearly resident or nonresident license and a striped-bass stamp (just in case you nail one, and you will...).

Guides: Fish First Guide Service, Doug Lovell and Leo Siren, PO Box 7215, Berkeley CA 94707, phone 510-526-1937; Pacific Adventures Guide Service, Mike Costello, 18582 Olive Street, Woodbridge, CA 95258; Prime Time Guide Service, Dan Blanton, 14720 Amberwood Lane, Morgan Hill, CA 94037, phone 408-778-0602

Maps/charts: Fish-n-Map Co. available at most shops and marinas for around 6 dollars.

Monterey Bay Potpourri

A good fish-finder graph is important when trying to locate suspended schools of rock bass over reefs and pinacles. Once a school is located, drop over a bright marker buoy to mark the spot and start casting. Use the countdown method to locate the depth of willing fish.
Inset: Schooling rock bass will hover near the surface during overcast mornings and are easily reachable with a fly.

I t was a perfect morning to be on Monterey Bay with a fly rod. Although it was only mid-August, the surface was as glassy as a mill pond in October with only a hint of swell to remind you that you were, indeed, standing in a skiff on the Pacific Ocean. A high layer of fog tented the bay with a grey veil. There wasn't a hint of a breeze to cause a labored cast, and the sun was just breaking over the coastal range, piercing the fog bank, washing the surface with warm hues of gold and amber. Sunbursts ricocheted off the windows of the half dozen cars negotiating the curves of West Cliff Drive on their way into the coastal town of Santa Cruz, its boardwalk and famous roller coaster still lighted and clearly visible not two miles distant. Small boats bobbed all around mine for as far as I could see, craft ranging from bright yellow, wooden rental skiffs, to rubber inflatables and center-consoles. Most had fly-anglers standing on their decks or squatting on their seats; many had as many as three long rods bent simultaneously, humping under the strain of hefty Pacific rock bass.

Swirls, busts and boils made by feeding bass could be seen here and there and my fish-finder graph had a school of fish marked that stretched off the screen. I knew it was going to be another great day on Monterey Bay. "Yeah! We're in the Bucket, guys!" I said, as I tossed over a brightly colored marker buoy with one hand while grabbing my 9-weight from the rack with the other. My companions, Bob Von Raesfeld and Server Sadik didn't need a New York second to follow suit. Within minutes Bob was lip-gaffing a four-pounder, followed shortly by Server and then moi. We were into them!

Monterey Bay, California may well provide the best marine fly-rodding to be found anywhere along this nation's temperate coastline. It certainly offers one of the most diverse flyrod fisheries, hosting a variety of species from early spring until late fall or early winter, depending upon the arrival of winter storms.

Knowledgeable fly-anglers have shots at rock bass, striped bass, white sea bass, halibut, salmon, bonito, mackerel, blue sharks, thresher sharks, jack smelt and surf perch. Depending upon the month, many of these species are available simultaneously, often only requiring a short move to other regions of the bay to find them. You may be flogging the rock bass over a rocky pinnacle a mile offshore, move a half mile farther and be into king salmon, or a move to nearshore kelp beds or protected coves with sandy beaches could have you locking horns with a white sea bass, halibut or a striped bass.

Flyfishing diversity: the hallmark of Monterey Bay!

Above: Olive rock bass are similar in appearance to largemouth bass and love bright flies.

Left: A brace of hefty 8-pounders, great sport on an 8- or 9-weight fly rod.

Rock Bass

I took my first Monterey Bay flyrod fish on a foggy day more than three decades ago. It was a hefty olive rock bass of around eight pounds. It fought better than your average largemouth bass and was a helluva lot easier to entice. I probably landed more than a hundred rock bass that day, a mix of olives, blues and blacks, all good sized and eager to eat flies. Fishing a brace of flies, I was consistently into doubles, which put a mean bend in my old glass rod. Two fat bass heading off in opposing directions simultaneously, pulled like hell and provided me

Above: Fish a fly deep enough to scratch the reef and you might score a ling cod.

Right: Light House Point and Seal Rock.

with incredible sport. I'll always be grateful to my old friend, the late Myron Gregory, a western flyfishing and fly-casting legend, for introducing me to fly-rodding for Pacific rock bass back in the early 1960s. I've never grown tired of catching them and look forward to several outings a year.

There are more than 50 varieties of these marine bass, which are not really a true bass, but are very similar to freshwater black bass in all the ways that count.

Monterey Bay hosts several species of rock bass but the most important are the olives, blues and blacks. There is also the occasional vermillion rock fish, more flamboyant than Dolly Parton, and only rewarded to those who are willing to scratch the reef top using weighted flies and lead-core shooting heads. The calico bass, probably the strongest of all the kelp basses, is an occasional added bonus, ranging up from southern regions when bay water temperatures push into the sixties.

Another bonus fish available to those who fish their flies deep enough to give them the bends, is the ling cod, one of the ugliest critters to ever terrorize a reef. They are definitely the bad boys on the block! It's a fish that thinks with its stomach, which means they are always hungry and no fly is too large! More than one fly-fisher has had a two-pound rock bass turn into a 20-pound ling cod.

There are three regions of Monterey Bay that produce excellent fly-fishing for reef-dwelling species. One of the best is located within sight of the Santa Cruz Municipal Wharf. It is Santa Cruz reef which stretches from Point Santa Cruz to Natural Bridges State Park, a distance of about three miles. Here, the best fishing occurs over submerged pinnacle tops, ranging in depth from 40 to 65 feet.

Classed as "bottom fish" by many, rock bass are usually found within the first 10 to 15 feet of the water column, except on the brightest days when currents are raging. Even then, many will still hover from mid-depth to 10 or 15 feet off bottom. On calm, overcast days hordes of bass will be feeding on or very near the top and can be easily taken on surface flies. The beauty of this area is that it is only a short run from the Santa Cruz small-craft harbor for those with their own boats; or from the Muni wharf, where it's even a shorter run from a rented, seaworthy wooden skiff.

Another productive reef and kelp bed area, which can also be easily reached by anglers casting from a rental boat, is just east of the Capitola pier, where boats can be rented from Capitola Bait and Tackle located on the Capitola pier. The kelp beds to the west of the pier, off Soquel Point, are also productive. All of the above-mentioned species can be taken from Capitola Bay, depending upon time of year.

There is also some excellent rock-bass fishing to be had in the Spanish Harbor area just outside of Monterey, south of Point Pinos. Being outside the protected bay, however, you'll need to watch the weather and water conditions.

The reef species season runs from June until late October, with August, September and October being prime time. Tune in to fishing reports, especially those provided by various Internet magazines and flyfishing-oriented websites covering the bay.

White Sea Bass

Monterey Bay's white sea bass—there is both bad and good news. The bad news: shortly after the Second World War, Monterey Bay's viable white sea bass fishery went the way of its sardine—commercially fished to near extinction. The good news: due to a white sea bass stocking program underway in Southern California, we are seeing many more white sea bass back in Monterey

Bay. About 5 years ago in May and June, for example, friends and I got into them on fly big time! Most of the fish I took were juveniles ranging from 24 to 30 inches (must be 28 inches long to legally take), but a good friend, Jose Silva, landed many that ranged from 20 to more than 30 pounds. He complained to me of having aching arms afterward. Yeah, like I cried a tear...

These fish love to roam the edges of the kelp forests and often school, chasing bait in narrow channels or in large openings within the kelp beds, many of which can be more than 200 or 300 feet in diameter, which make

Above: The boat ramp at the Santa Cruz small-craft harbor.

Middle: A flamboyant vermillion rock bass, a fairly rare catch on a fly-rod. You must fish a fly deep to catch one.

Lower: The most productive days are when it's overcast with high fog.

them a perfect "near-shore" target for fly-fishers. Look for them along the kelp in 15 to 35 feet of water from Point Santa Cruz to Natural Bridges State Park out of Santa Cruz, and from Soquel Point to Sea Cliff in Soquel Cove, almost within a long cast of the Capitola pier.

Whites love squid and Monterey Bay is lousy with squid. In fact, the schools of fish we found would only take squid patterns fished fairly deep (15 to 30 count) on lead-core shooting heads. They were as selective as any trout! My Sea Arrow Squid and Kate Howe's Calimari were deadly! But, having these flies armed with wire weed guards to prevent snagging on kelp fronds would make them even more efficient. They also

eat anchovies and sardines and having a good general baitfish simulator is advisable. Patterns such as the Flashtail Clouser, Flashtail Whistler, Sar-Mul-Mac, Lefty's Deceiver and others work well fished on shooting heads and integrated heads ranging in density from intermediate to lead core.

These fish are within reach of both private skiffs and rental boats during the months of April, May and June, but seem to be around much longer now and reports indicate there might be a year-round fishery. Late spring through high summer offers the fly-angler the best opportunity, though. We are still learning about them. Keep an ear tuned for the word that the white sea bass are in!

Striped Bass

Striped bass terrorize bait on many of the beaches in Monterey Bay from Capitola to the mouth of the Salinas River below Moss Landing, and are available to fly-anglers casting from beach or boat. Best time: late May through October, with June and July peaking the season.

The water in Soquel Cove, which ranges from Capitola to Seacliff, is often extremely calm and can be alive with sheeting baitfish and diving birds. Great action is often found on beaches like New Brighton, Pot Belly, Seacliff, Rio Del Mar, Manresa and Sunset. One of my favorite striper beats is the South Jetty Beach at Moss Landing, between the south jetty and the Old Kaiser Pier. Though rare, bass in the 40-pound class have been taken by fly-casters covering this stretch. Stripers in the 20-pound class are not uncommon, and I have taken them to 25 pounds on fly, casting toward the beach from my center-console skiff.

the Steamer Lane surfing area between Pt. Santa Cruz and the Municipal pier; the beach west of Black Point; and all of the beaches between Capitola beach and Sea Cliff, including those adjacent to both sides of the Pajaro River. South Jetty Beach at Moss Landing: great fly-rod halibut turf.

Salmon

I've taken many good kings and a few silvers on flies from Monterey Bay during the past couple of decades. It's a fact, though, that you'll catch far more with a mooched anchovy than on the best-designed fly. Unlike the often extremely productive river fly-rod action for

Above: White sea bass have returned to Monterey Bay. This one is a juvenile, but there are plenty of very large fish around.

Middle: A bank of dense fog can move in quickly, or be there from day's start. A good GPS unit and a compass are necessary for safety's sake.

Lower: A fly-rodder works on a nice one from a rental boat in Capitola cove.

California Halibut

Gill-netters and trawlers have devastated fish stocks along all coastlines of this country. Where ever the net-ters have been voted out, however, suppressed fish stocks have recovered amazingly fast.

California halibut had gone the way of the eastern striper, Florida snook and Texas redfish, before these states kicked the netters out. But now, like those recov-ering species, California halibut are making a pro-nounced come-back all along the California coast since our commercial trawlers were given the boot. While usually targeted by gear and bait fishers, fly-rodders are sticking a fair share of these flatties, particularly along the traditional halibut beaches of Monterey Bay. Most fly-anglers are fishing from a boat, although, beach cast-ers score too.

Halibut prefer sandy beaches in water ranging from eight to about 15 feet in depth. They are voracious feed-ers that lay buried to their eyeballs in sand, waiting to ambush any hapless baitfish (or your fly) that swims by. While it is best to plow the sandy bottom with your fly, halibut will move a considerable distance for a meal, and I have taken them from deeper water, nearer the surface than the bottom.

Excellent halibut beats include the sandy beaches found between Natural Bridges and Point Santa Cruz; at

kings along the north coast of California and Oregon, ocean fish are more easily taken with mooched bait or trolled gear.

However, you can take these great fish from the Monterey salt chuck on a variety of anchovy-simulating, shrimp and squid flies. The best tactic is to use a type-four to -six or lead-core shooting head,. Cast ahead of the drift let the line sink to the level of the fish and then just inch it along, almost mooching it. Takes will usually be subtle but can also be wrist-wrenching. While ocean salmon can be taken using faster, staccato retrieves, more will be hooked by using the "no retrieve" mooching technique.

Your greatest opportunity to score on Monterey salmon will be during the months of June, July and early August, when anchovy schools will be in shallow water trying to spawn with salmon hot on their tails.

Sharks: Blues and Threshers

Shark stocks worldwide have been pounded to all-time lows by commercial fishers for food, fins and so-called cancer-abating medicines. Pacific blue sharks and threshers are no exception.

Despite declines, though, Monterey Bay is still famous for its productive fly-fishery for blue sharks, a sport pioneered by Bob Edgley and Lawrence Summers back in the early 1970s. It is still not unusual to have 10 to 15 "smilies," as we call them, encircling the boat, biting the prop or chum basket, or just cruising the chum slick looking for a meal. This is sight-fishing that spawns elemental fear, while simultaneously stoking your fire for maximum fly-rod adventure. You can pick your fish, ranging from 30-pounders to 150-pound rod-busters. It is a great way to tune up for fly-rod battles with big game, like the billfish or tuna species, particularly if you have never engaged them. It's exciting fishing that won't cost the family fortune in order to participate. Best time: summer through late fall. Best area: At the edge of the Monterey Trench (just offshore of Moss Landing), the deepest subterranean canyon on the Pacific Rim, in water depths ranging from 100 to 200 feet. Of course they can be found off Santa Cruz or Capitola in the same depths, but you'll have a longer run.

Above: Striped bass run the beaches of Monterey during summer and fall.

Left: Angler Gil Santos of Santa Cruz, displays a nice white sea bass taken on a squid pattern near the kelp in Capitola Cove.

Thresher sharks are plentiful in Monterey Bay, too. When it comes to aerial antics, they are right there with billfish and tarpon and will give you a run to boot. While not as easy to hook as a blue, they can be taken on a fly, particularly when they gang up on huge schools of anchovies that aggregate close to shore for spawning during the months of June, July and August.

Some of the best thresher beats are found in the Santa Cruz area inside of mile buoy, often just off the mouth of the small craft harbor, and just outside of Elkhorn Slough at Moss Landing. Look for "jumpers"; and when you see one, get there pronto and cast an anchovy- or sardine-simulating fly (armed with a single-strand wire bite leader and lots of flash) into the area. Fish it slow, while occasionally letting it drop and flutter downward like an injured baitfish. Threshers use their incredibly long tails as clubs to stun prey and key on injured, descending bait. An intermediate to type II sinking shooting head, looped to 100 feet of Scientific Anglers new Mastery saltwater shooting line would be a perfect line choice.

Bonito, Pacific Mackerel and Other Itinerants

Some of the greatest fly-fishing Monterey Bay has to offer occurs during *El Niño* years, when the bay's waters warm into the mid-60s. Taking advantage of this phenomenon requires the fly-rodder to maintain a vigilant ear for word that bonito, jumbo Pacific mackerel, and Pacific barracuda are in. When this happens, cancel all plans for other fly-flinging and head for the bay!

Above: Del Brown with a schoolie taken on a Whistler cast from a skiff just outside the surfline.

Right: Ed Given displays a nice California halibut. These fish can be taken on flies cast from boats or from the beach.

The bonito will be found wherever the bait is thickest, from near shore to a mile or so from the beach. Ditto for big macs. 'Cuda will run the shoreline, over sandy stretches, with the Capitola area producing some of the best bites. Short, single-wire bite leaders are a must for 'cuda, but are not required for bonito and mackerel.

Bonito will run in size from three to 15 pounds. In fact, Bob Edgley still holds the world record for Pacific bonito in the 12-pound tippet class with a gorilla weighing 15 1/2 pounds, a fish he took from the bay on my Sea Arrow Squid during an *El Niño* day, on September 15, 1972.

Jack Smelt and Surf Perch

Tougher than any trout, jack smelt are found in huge numbers in Monterey Bay. They range in size from just

inches to a couple of pounds, and are a scream on four- and five-weight rods. They can even be taken on small, tan-colored dry flies.

One of the best ways to get into these fish is to chum them up with a block of frozen ground chum (anchovies, etc.). In fact they are always the first to show in the slick when chumming for sharks. Flies should resemble bits and pieces of chum and be white or tan, size 10 to 14. A tuft of white marabou around the hook will suffice for your wets; and a hank of deer hair tied caddis-style will do it for dries. If larger specimens are encountered, mini-streamers and tiny bucktails will produce.

Surf perch species run all the beaches from Capitola to Monterey. They feed on a variety of crustaceans, like sand fleas, small crabs and shrimp. Flies need only be simple, chenille-bodied comets, small Clousers, Buggers or shrimp patterns, and while somber ties will take fish, bright red or orange seems to push their strike button best. One of the top fly patterns is Jay Murakoshi's Rusty Squirrel Clouser. Fly lines: some rave over sink-tips while others swear by fast-sinking shooting heads. Both work! A stripping basket is a must.

Monterey Bay is an incredible place for the marine fly-fisher and it should only get better if current conservation practices continue. But it isn't just a great piece of fly-fishing water for locals, it's also a great place for visitors on vacation, with attractions like the Monterey Bay Aquarium, Cannery Row, Pebble Beach, 17-Mile Drive, Fisherman's Wharf, many fine restaurants, Santa Cruz boardwalk, its famous roller coaster and much more. Located within two hours or less from major Bay Area airports, Monterey Bay is an incredibly easy place to get to. It has many excellent hotels, and several good campgrounds close by, a couple of them are right on good surf

Above: The author displays a jumbo Pacific mackerel, great fun on a light fly rod.

Right: Blue sharks roam Monterey Bay in good numbers and are targeted by fly-anglers.

perch and striper beaches. So if you are inclined, bring the family to Monterey Bay for a great vacation, and while mom (if she doesn't fly-fish) and the kids are taking in the sights, you can be enjoying Monterey Bay on the fly.

Planning An Outing

More on Flies and Gear: Other productive flies for Monterey Bay include, Blanton's Punch Series, Blanton's Sea Arrow Squid, Blanton's Flashtail Whistlers, Flashtail Clousers, Blanton's Sar-Mul-Mac, Lefty's Deceivers, Trey Combs Sea Habit Deceivers, Horner Shrimp patterns in brown, green and orange, and similar types in sizes ranging from 4 to 4/0, in a variety of colors.

Rods range from 3-weights for jack smelt and mackerel to 12-weight sticks for sharks. Seven- to 10-weight rods work well for rock bass to stripers and white sea bass. Shooting heads ranging from floaters to lead core provide the greatest versatility. Mono-type shooting lines are best for getting deep.

Where to Stay: myriad hotels in Santa Cruz and Monterey, or camp at several private and state campgrounds. Check with the local Chambers of Commerce for current information.

Guide Service: Currently the only guide service available for nearshore fishing from a boat that specializes in fly-fishing is Prime Time on the Fly Guide Service, with me, Captain Dan Blanton: 14720 Amberwood Lane, Morgan Hill, CA 95037, phone: 408-778-0602, e-mail: flasht@ix.netcom.com. For beach guiding contact Monterey Bay Fly Fishing Guide Service : Jim Novak 126 Getchell Street, Santa Cruz, CA. 95060 e-mail: jim@mbflyfishing.com California DFG guide license# 704102-02 or Ben Taylor 124 Palo Verde Terrace, Santa Cruz, CA, 95060, e-mail: ben@mbflyfishing.com, California DFG guide license# 704170-02.

Beach Clinics: Ken Hanley and Jay Murakoshi conduct excellent beach/surf fly fishing clinics. Contact: Adventures Beyond, P.O. Box 3239, Freemont, CA 94539, phone: 510-657-4847

Boat Rentals: You can rent boats from Capitola Bait and Tackle on the Capitola pier, phone: 831-462-2208, or off the Santa Cruz wharf, Santa Cruz boat rentals, phone: 831-423-1739. Call for current rates and related information.

The Return of Monterey Bay White Sea Bass

Above: The author displays a juvenile white sea bass taken on a squid fly.

Inset: White sea bass have a penchant for dining on squid.

I t was mid-June, 1996, and I had just learned via the local flyfishing grapevine that a couple of Santa Cruz fly-rodders were scoring well with white sea bass along Monterey Bay's, Capitola kelp beds, well inside Soquel Point. They weren't giant fish, mostly schoolies, just under the minimum size length of 28 inches. I was told they only wanted squid flies, and with the right one, action could be fast. Monterey Bay is loaded with squid, candy to a white sea bass, and I had a great squid fly.

I've always known that white sea bass, more commonly associated with the Southern California salt chuck, did frequent Monterey Bay. Jack Daniels, a long passed-away fly-fishing buddy, loved to tell tales of the huge schools of bruiser-sized white sea bass that used to call Monterey Bay home until they were picked clean by the commercial netters shortly after World War II.

During the past decade, I had heard rumors that a few whites were back, but reports of big fish landed by bait and gear anglers increased during the last few years. In fact, I had learned that my good friend JoseSilva, a Peruvian transplant, who lives to fly-fish, had also taken some trophy white sea bass on fly from Monterey Bay kelp forests during the prior two seasons—fish in the 20- to 40-pound range, and had his clock cleaned a couple of times by even larger fish. This, plus the most recent report of schoolie action, really stoked my fire and plans were promptly made to give these Monterey Bay white sea bass a try.

Gil Santos and I launched his Whaler at the Santa Cruz small-craft harbor, running a few miles down the coast to Soquel Point, and into Capitola Cove. It took us awhile to locate the school of juvie whites we'd heard about. We started our search with lead-core shooting heads and Sea Arrow Squid flies, about half way between Soquel Point and the Capitola Wharf, working over 30 to 40 feet of water within a cast of the dense kelp forest that parallels the precipitous coastline from Soquel Point to the beach.

Electric-motoring slowly along the beds, casting both toward the kelp and to open water, it took about an hour to locate the first bass. It came from open water near where the kelp beds formed a corner, after a count-down of about 25. The grab was nearly identical to the way a striper hits and the fight was similar, although I thought I had connected with a much larger fish than it actually was, suggesting that white sea bass tug a little harder than a striped bass for their size. The fish was 27 inches long and though not a monster, I was as happy as a duck dog in November with my first-ever white sea bass on a fly.

Within a few minutes Gil scored his introductory white of almost identical size and he too was impressed with the critter's strength and striking looks. "What a tough little beauty!" he exclaimed. "I can't imagine what a 40-pounder would be like."

We kept working toward the Capitola wharf, into shallower water, finally locating the mother load. The large school of whites we'd been told about where terrorizing squid in a half-acre open area within the kelp beds, in water ranging from 18 to 22 feet deep. The fish weren't top-side since the sun was high and the squid deep. A count of 25 to 30, with an erratic, medium speed retrieve, produced best.

Above: Working from his skiff and casting to lanes in the kelp, Jose Silva scored this nice white sea bass on a Lefty's Deceiver.

Left: Jose Silva may have been the first to score a Monterey white sea bass on a fly.

For more than an hour and a half, action was steady with a hit or fish coming every few casts. We tried different fly styles, mostly baitfish simulators, but the word had been right on—they only wanted white squid flies that day. All of the fish looked as though they had been cloned, ranging from 24 to 30 inches long. Most were sub-legal size but none the less a blast to catch and release, with the hope that a monster would inhale our fly next cast. It was a memorable day, leaving us both

The Return of Monterey Bay White Sea Bass

with a true sense that a thriving white seabass fishery might be in store for Monterey Bay fly-fishers.

The white sea bass is actually not a true sea bass but rather a member of the corvina and weakfish family—a close relative of the giant totuava. Their natural range extends from Chile to Alaska, but it is rarely found north of San Francisco, favoring warmer waters of southern climes. While they can attain a size of 80 pounds and four feet, fish ranging from sub-legal to 40 or so pounds are most common. They are found both in open water and near kelp beds, spawn in spring and summer and are most abundant from May to September in California, although I'm not sure of the entire Monterey Bay season. Males spawn at about 24 inches in length, females at about 27 inches. They feed on baitfishes, crustaceans and squid.

The body color of a white sea bass is gray to blue on the back, silvery on the sides, pecs a dusky coloration. They are really a handsome species, long and slim, much like a large corvina. They do have teeth but don't have long canines in the upper jaw.

You are required to have a landing net of at least 18 inches in diameter aboard when fishing for salmon, and I would expect the same requirement when targeting whites because of the minimum length size limit. However, I personally dislike the use of nets. Handling these fish roughly or for any length of time can cause body slime removal which invariably leads to bacterial infection and fungus which can kill the fish. A better landing method is to use a Boga grip or similar device, which is much easier on the fish and keeps your fingers clear of sharp teeth.

What May Be Bringing Them Back

I'm not sure of the exact reason why both school-sized white sea bass and adults are showing up again in larger numbers in Monterey Bay and along the coast as far

Above to upper right: Gil Santos retrieves his squid fly near the kelp, hooks up and brings a nice bass to hand.

Far right bottom: Capitola cove hosts a thick kelp forest where white sea bass love to roam, seeking squid and baitfish.

north as Half Moon Bay. My guess is that it's a combination of positive actions and interactions by various Southern California user/conservation groups, state and federal agencies. The elimination of gill and trawl nets along the California coast certainly is a factor. But the establishment of the Leon Raymond Hubbard Marine Fish Hatchery in Carlsbad, along with legislation that formed the Ocean Resources Enhancement Hatchery Program (OREHP), are more likely the greatest contributors.

The Hatchery Program

The white seabass hatchery program was the brainchild of devout angler, Milt Shedd, Chairman of the AFTCO tackle company, co-founder of Sea World, Inc., and the founder of the Hubbs-Sea World Research Institute. Through his auspices, and the combined efforts of his son, Bill, biologist Don Kent, the California D.F.G., the United Anglers of Southern California, the Sport

Fishing Association of California, the American Sportfishing Association, State legislators and various fishing clubs and individuals in the angling community, Milt's dream of a saltwater hatchery program became reality. By the end of 1997, the Hubbard Marine Fish hatchery along with 11 grow-out facilities where in operation with the capacity to release some 400,000 white sea bass annually.

Grow-out Facilities a Major Factor

The grow-out facility program was conceived by Bill Shedd of UASC. The plan was to develop a series of grow-out operations along the Southern California coast, run by fishing clubs, with leadership coming from UASC, including future funding and program direction. The model and first grow-out facility, was developed by and successfully operated in Oxnard by Jim Donlon.

48   *Fly Fishing California's Great Waters*

With both Jim and UASC's help, ten more grow-out facilities were established. Grow-out facilities now in operation are: Balboa Angling Club; Catalina Island Grow-Out; Dana Angling Club; Hope; King Harbor Marlin Club; Marina Del Ray Anglers; San Diego Oceans Foundation; Santa Barbara S.E.A.; Southwestern Yacht Club and Ventura County Chapter UAC.

Brood Stock

United Anglers of Southern California and the Sportfishing Association of California (SAC) and other members of the sportfishing community play an important role in obtaining brood stock for the hatchery. Members of SAC, along with other dedicated boat owners and anglers, devote large chunks of their fishing season to collecting brood stock.

The white sea bass are spawned and their eggs are hatched at the Hubbs research facility. The larvae are grown until about 2.5 inches long at which time they are delivered to the grow-out facilities. They are fed and nurtured until they reach a length of about eight inches and are then released after being tagged with a small, coded wire head implant, embedded in a gill cover just below the eye. About ten percent are also tagged with external "anchor" tags.

The success of this program and its special uniqueness is the direct result of volunteer involvement by sport anglers who spend huge amounts of personal time raising the bass before release. For more information on the white seabass hatchery program and how you can become involved, call the United Anglers of Southern California at (714) 840-0227.

Are the white sea bass we're now catching in Monterey Bay Hubbs hatchery fish? I can't answer that. I've talked with Southern California DFG marine biologist, Stephen Wertz about that possibility. He was delighted to learn we were catching juvenile whites in Monterey Bay, but said without recovering the tags from legal length fish, no one could be sure. Most of the fish tagged since the inception of the stocking program, are just now reaching legal length and a tag collection system hasn't been coordinated at this time. Steve did point out, however, that if an angler catches a sub-legal fish or one intended for release that is wearing an external anchor tag, the Department would appreciate receiving the information off the tag, along with its weight, where and when the fish was caught. Call or send the information to the California Department of Fish and Game, marine resources division: 330 Golden Shore, Suite 50, Long Beach, CA 90802. Phone: (562) 590-5161.

Locating Fish

Because I'm just learning about this fishery, I can't point to all the areas Monterey white sea bass roam. The most consistent spot seems to be along the kelp forest from Soquel Point, north into Capitola Cove to nearly the end of the kelp beds, a long cast from the Capitola Pier. They

The Return of Monterey Bay White Sea Bass

Jose Silva and others have also scored on them outside of Capitola Bay, west along the kelp beds toward Santa Cruz. Reports indicate that whites are also found from Point Santa Cruz to Natural Bridges in or near the kelp. And while not Monterey Bay, large whites have been taken by anglers fishing out of Half Moon Bay; and a large school of good-sized fish have been encountered inside San Franciso Bay the last couple of years.

There is little kelp from Capitola Bay until you reach the city of Monterey, with most of it south of the harbor and along Cannery Row. It is likely that white sea bass frequent these forests as they migrate up the coast.

Like I said before, the bass tend to key on kelp and are often found within the larger openings, but they can also occasionally be found busting bait in open water well outside the kelp edges in deeper water. They may also be keying on squid deeper in the column from just a few feet down to as deep as 30 feet or more. It pays to keep a vigilant eye peeled for working birds and surface eruptions,but don't hesitate to ply the depths as well. Use your depth recorder to find bait and fish.

Tackle, Flies and Techniques

Again, we are still learning, but it seems appropriate to think BIG FISH when selecting gear. True, a 7- to 9-weight stick is just right for schoolies, but what if you get nailed by Big Moe? Anything lighter than a 10-weight and the fish will crochet your line through the kelp, parting you from line and fly in a nanosecond. I personally use a 10- or 11-weight rod armed with a 12-weight, type 4 to 6, or a 30-foot lead-core shooting head, looped to a Scientific Anglers Mastery .035 coated shooting line. The coated line lets me fish moderately deep but provides a degree of control when I need to lean on a fish hard in order to turn it from kelp. For reaching deep feeders, say down to 30 feet, a mono-type shooting line such as Rio's clear intermediate shooting line in .030 diameter is a better choice.

Reels: I prefer true, large-arbor styles, such as Tibor's Everglades, although any reel of similar quality will certainly suffice, including those with standard-

Above: Frank Bertaina displays an 18-pound white sea bass taken on a Flashtail Clouser. These fish reach a size of over 90 pounds.

Upper right: Casting along the kelp beds at Natural Bridges State Park area.

Opposite: Because white sea bass can attain huge sizes, it's best to use rods/reels rated from 9- to 11-weight; reels should have an excellent drag and ample backing capacity.

are also found in good numbers from Monterey harbor to Lovers Point when the squid are spawning. Stan Pleskenas scored the 16-pound tippet world record from that area in September 2001 with a 38.9-pound white sea bass. Fishing for white sea bass often shines off the mouth of the Pajaro River as well.

Fly Fishing California's Great Waters

sized spools. A good drag and ample backing are principle considerations.

In order to cover all bases, carry a good selection of both squid and baitfish patterns in a variety of sizes. My Sea Arrow Squid is an excellent, proven pattern; ditto for Kate and Bill Howe's Calimari squid fly and Jay Murakoshi has a wonderful squid pattern he calls the Llama Hair Squid. The Sar-Mul-Mac in sardine and anchovy are superb in sizes ranging from 3/0 to 4/0, as are Sea Habits and Lefty's Deceivers. Flashtail Whistlers and Clousers are also good choices. It is advisable to use a short bite leader of 30- or 40-pound mono for abrasion insurance. Leaders: 20-pound class, Bimini twist leaders for maximum breaking strength, no longer than about seven feet in length, including a 30- or 40-pound butt section.

What about presentation and retrieves? Of course I'm still learning but here is what seems to ring their bell: Let the fly sink to their feeding level and then work it back with a slow to medium fast, erratic pull. Hits came at any time and follows to the surface were frequent. Other anglers I've talked with experienced pretty much the same when the fish were down and feeding on squid. Others, though, have experienced surface or near-surface action, with strikes coming without having to sink the fly much. Often slow-sinking lines outshine deep-diving densities. Smart anglers will cover the entire water column using the countdown method to determine the feeding/strike zone, while keeping eyes peeled for surface action.

The Season

Again, I'm not sure exactly when the first whites start to show up in our neighborhood, but I'm guessing that the season will range from May through summer into fall. We took our fish during June. To keep current with information about white seabass action, give Ed Burrell, owner of Capitola Boat & Bait, a call at (831)462-2208 or monitor my website bulletin board at www.danblanton.com.

Boats and Conditions

Monterey Bay, especially Capitola Bay, during early summer through fall can be placid and serene. It can also get downright ugly, particularly in afternoon when the wind is up with a big tide running. If you run to Capitola Bay from the Santa Cruz small-craft harbor, keep a vigilant eye toward Soquel Point for increasing late-morning and afternoon wind, lest you find wild water as you round the point, heading home at fishing's end. Accordingly, a larger boat is best, something ranging from 16 to 20 feet, one that can still be controlled with an electric trolling motor. If you don't have a boat or access to one, you're still not out of it. You can rent a skiff from Capitola Boat & Bait, only a half mile from the action area, and never have to worry about the wind or swells or washing it down. Call ahead for reservations.

Since that first encounter with Gil Santos, I've spent many hours on Monterey Bay pursuing white sea bass. I've experienced some great successes and some failures—one day you're a hero, the next day you're a goat. That's fishing. The most exciting thing, though, is that the white sea bass are growing both in numbers and size in Monterey Bay and I'm hopeful the fishery will continue its incredible recovery.

CHAPTER

A Legacy of Blues

A pair of blue sharks gliding into the chum slick, one taking the fly.

Inset: Four on at once!

They appear in the chum slick with a startling suddenness, gliding in on long, cobalt pectorals; powerful, yet beautiful and graceful, almost aeronautical. Blue sharks, they always engender quickness of breath and an uncontrollable surge of adrenaline. This is sight-fishing; the kind of saltwater fly-rodding that stirs extreme excitement, mixed with elemental fear and hair-raising anxiety, the result of meeting "jaws" face-to-face, close enough to touch.

Indeed, when blue sharks ascend upon the source of the scent molecules that have drawn them from the depths, they come without hesitation, fear or reserve. They are guided only by instinct, an instinct to feed on whatever is producing the irresistible scent. They come alone or in pods. I've had as many as 15 circling the boat simultaneously—an awesome sight! They test bite the prop, bump the transom with their long blue snouts, and grab the chum basket in a cavernous mouth, serrated, triangular teeth snagging in the wire mesh, glistening deadly white, as the denizen thrashes madly trying to free itself. I have reached down and touched the dorsal of a 150-pounder gliding by so close that its sandpaper-like hide left cobalt scratches on my boat's white hull. When the angler finally regains focus, he or she picks the fish with which to do battle. For me, it's always the biggest of the lot; the one with the torque of a steam engine and the speed of a quarter horse. The one that will challenge my tackle, knots and rigging, along with my fish-fighting skills—to the limit! I am rarely disappointed.

Fly-fishing for blue sharks is biggame angling with all the desirable elements of the our sport without the usual high-dollar sacrifice. It is a fishery that is readily accessible to fly-anglers on both coasts of this country, as well as internationally—blues are oceanic, like many other shark species. When chummed properly, taking them on a fly is the closest thing to guaranteed fishing I know, and I've witnessed as many as four anglers hooked-up simultaneously during a hot bite. Despite that, though, they sometimes don't always eat and have to be coaxed into taking the fly. Once one does ingest your feathered offering, however, and the steel is slammed home, be prepared for an incredible shower of spray as the critter rips the surface apart in protest, before streaking off on a long surface sprint that will test the drag and mettle of the best big-game fly reel. Backing will melt from your spool so quickly you'll fear that you haven't enough. The final throngs of the battle will test your physical condition, including the mettle of your mind. The really big ones can be proverbial "Ball Busters", leaving you with screaming muscles you never dreamed you had.

Above: Pioneer of fly-fishing for blue sharks, Bob Edgley displays a world-record, 150-pounder taken around 1973.

Left: A frozen block of ground-up chum placed in a wire basket and hung over the side works best; a big blue takes the fly right in the chum slick.

History

It all started in 1972 when Bob Edgley and Lawrence Summers, both of San Jose, California, decided to cash in on what was obviously then, an untapped sport fishery in Monterey Bay. They noticed, when out chasing salmon, bonito, mackerel and other bay gamesters, a tremendous number of large blue sharks cruising the surface of the bay, either prowling for sustenance, or sunning themselves. Bob and Larry realized that the possibility of a colossal but unknown fly-rod fishery existed very close to shore, within sight of a major metropolitan area. All they had to do was figure out how to get them to eat flies.

It took almost two years of experimentation but the final formula to consistent success was to chum the fish into a feeding mood, drawing them to the back of a seaworthy boat, presenting the angler with an opportunity to drop a fly in front of a near-frenzied blue, which may have, just moments before, tried to eat the prop. What worked best for Bob and Larry, was to hang a frozen block of oily ground-up fish parts (anchovies, mackerel, salmon carcasses, etc.), over the side in a wire-mesh basket, letting the warm sea water automatically thaw and dispense the chum bits and oil molecules as the boat drifted with wind and tide. Once the chum slick was started, they were committed to it for at least an hour. Often the first blue would show within minutes. Other times it would take the better part of an hour; but come they would, and often in great numbers.

Hard, Messy Work

They hand-ground their chum using a meat grinder—hard work at best (I personally hate the job and today I purchase commercially-produced chum) being sure they had at least six half-gallon milk cartons of chum for each outing. They didn't want to run out of chum too soon, or worse, before the critters arrived! Mixing a little water and cooking oil with the mess seems to make the chum more effective. Some anglers grind fresh chum on the spot, but I personally think it is far more effective to use hand-ground frozen chum or commercial vacuum-packed or canned chum. I'd rather have a fly-rod grip in my hand than the handle of a grinder when I'm on the bay, particularly if the swell is up, if you get my meaning.

The Mighty Mites

The first to arrive in any slick are usually jack smelt and mackerel. They can be taken on any small white fly, size 10 for smelt, size 2s for mackerel, and are a blast to catch on trout-sized rods; and, when chunked into small pieces, make excellent appetizers for any shark moving up the slick. Toss a chunk over every few minutes but don't overdo it. Doing this usually guarantees any shark arriving at the transom will be ready to eat anything it sees drifting in the slick.

Presentation and Rigging

They found that casts would be short, usually under 20 feet, almost dappling; and retrieving the fly would not illicit a response. They had to dead-drift the fly in the currents as though it were a drifting chunk of bait. Accordingly flies were simple affairs, usually just a hank-of-hair and feathers of white or yellow about the same size as an anchovy. Today, many anglers use a white or yellow rabbit strip with a touch of red, brown or maroon in the flanks. Hooks are always bronze, ranging in size from 4/0 to 6/0, and a wire bite leader of at least 12 inches is required. Solid wire works best and many employ a barrel swivel between the bite and class leader, which helps prevent line-twist, since sharks often spiral toward bottom on their last-ditch run for freedom. The fly is connected using a haywire twist. Class leaders should be constructed using Bimini twist knots for 100% efficiency, and a hard mono such as Mason offers the greatest protection against abrasive hides and slicing pectorals.

Tackling Up

Today, most use a sinking shooting-head, usually a type 4, coupled to a coated, level shooting-line. Blues are not always right on top and being able to get down a few feet can mean the difference between success or failure; and since a sinking line is dramatically smaller in diameter than a floater, there is less line drag, which helps prevent line-drag break-offs. If a fish rolls up on the line, breaking off, heads are not as costly a loss. Still, sharks can often be enticed into taking a large popper, one usually made of foam, and having one outfit rigged with a floater can lead to great fun since it is a kick to watch a huge shark try to eat a popper. You won't believe it until you see it!

Rods need to be beefy! I wouldn't use anything less than an 11-weight, preferably a 12- to 13-weight for deepwater blue sharking. First runs are almost always on the surface but when it gets down to the slugfest, these fish will almost always sound, meaning you are going to have to put your back and rod butt into it—I mean really into it! No wimp rod is going to get the job done in respectable time. I've seen more than one rod blow up, failing under severe lifting pressure while the angler tried to pump a large fish from abysmal depths.

Fighting Tactics

Once hooked up, always play the angles, pulling the fish off balance when it is on or near the surface. Apply maximum pressure, all that your leader and rod can stand. Poor it on, to within ounces of the breaking strength of the tippet. Never let the shark rest. If it's not taking line, you should be gaining it. No standoffs allowed! Keep your rod low and to the side, not straight up between your eyes. The only exception to this rule is when the fish panics and sounds when it is close to the boat. Crowding it then will only make it spiral violently, wrapping your line around its body like gauze on a mummy—kiss off fish and line! Back off then, let the fish sound on an almost drag-free setting. It won't do the Bimini twist on you and will come right back to the surface so you can apply the heat again.

Landing Them

Most don't bother gaffing these brutes, opting instead to just carefully clip the wire, releasing them to fight again. This is the reason for using bronze hooks instead of cad-plated or stainless; bronze hooks rust out quickly. If you do decide to gaff a fish, be sure you have thoroughly

dispatched it before bringing it aboard—more than one "dead" shark has severely bitten someone!

Sharks do not seem to have pain-sensitive mouths and often return to feeding almost immediately after being released or broken off. I have personally hooked the same fish three different times during the same outing. It is really an ego-bashing to have a Big Moe continue feeding after you have set the hook with all the might your arms, back and rod could muster, not even realizing it has been hooked.

More on Tackle

Almost any quality large-capacity, true large-arbor reel will suffice. Line capacity and adequate drag is the key factor. Be sure to load on at least 300 yards of 30-pound Dacron or Micron. Backing is insurance and you'll often need it. The choice of direct-drive or anti-reverse is entirely up to you, although most would probably opt for direct-drive with dominant-hand cranking. This isn't trout-fishing, folks!

Don't Lose Your Chum Slick

All the backing in the world is sometimes not enough if you hook a real whopper in the century-weight class and have to follow the critter with the boat. Problem is, you don't want to have to start a new chum slick when the battle is over. One tactic that Edgley and Summers used was to toss out a marking buoy, a 3-foot dowel running through a block of foam, to which at one end was attached a lead sinker, and at the other, a hot-orange flag. When they had to chase a fish, this tip-up buoy was tossed out, marking the head of their slick so they could return and re-establish it quickly. Sharks would often be found milling around the buoy.

Where to Find Them

Blue sharks are pelagic and generally prefer deep water, although they are sometimes seen skimming the surface in 100 feet or less. One of the best areas to locate them in Monterey Bay is a couple of miles offshore of Elkhorn Slough at Moss Landing, which is at the apex of the bay.

Above: Beefy rods are required to lift blues from the depths once the long surface runs are over.

Left: A big blue about to be lip-gaffed; cutting the wire for release.

Opposite page: Fly rods can actually beat big fish faster than gear, if in skilled hands; single-strand wire is better than multi-strand.

Here is where the incredibly deep Monterey Trench comes closest to shore, and large numbers of blue sharks call the region home.

There are plenty of blue sharks in Southern California, too. In fact, Bob Edgley and Lawrence Summers were the first to fly-fish for blues and mako sharks in Southern California, using the same techniques they pioneered in Monterey Bay. Larry took the first mako shark, a 45-pounder, on a fly back in 1974. That Mako was followed by one caught by Yours Truly and then one stuck by Nick Curcione. These were boated in 1974 or 1975, I believe, using the exact tactics developed by Bob and Larry. Today, their techniques have not changed one microbe and work equally well for East Coast fly-rodders. In fact, Capt. Mike Hintlian, of Ipswich, Mass spent time with me many years ago, learning about West Coast Blue-sharking techniques, taking them to his home turf, proving they worked equally well there.

Bob Edgley and Lawrence Summers were true saltwater fly-rod pioneers; and while they both are still alive and kicking, they, like many others, have left us all a valuable legacy—the legacy of being able to fly-fish for two of the most intriguing and exciting sport fishes known to man: The blue and mako shark, both worthy of your time and tackle.

8
CHAPTER

Lakes of Giants

Being on the lakes early and late—the magic hours—can make a huge difference...

Inset: ...especially during high summer.

San Luis Reservoir and the O'Neill Forebay are arguably this country's top producers of giant, fly-caught landlocked striped bass. If you were looking to catch a world-record fly-caught landlocked striped bass and asked me what body of water would provide the best opportunity to do it, I'd hand you the answer in a heart beat: California's San Luis Reservoir and its equalizing basin, the O'Neill Forebay. But don't take my word for it—check the stats from the International Game Fish Association's world records book at right.

World Records
Bass, Striped—Landlocked

1 kg (2 lb.) 29 lb. 8 oz	San Luis Reservoir	Al Whitehurst
2 kg (4 lb.) 32 lb. 12 oz	San Luis Reservoir	Al Whitehurst
3 kg (6 lb.) 38 lb.	San Luis Reservoir	Len Bearden
4 kg (8 lb.) 39 lb. 8 oz	San Luis Reservoir	Al Whitehurst
6 kg (12 lb.) 40 lb. 4 oz	O'Neill Forebay	Al Whitehurst
8 kg (16 lb.) 54 lb. 8 oz	O'Neill Forebay	Al Whitehurst
10 kg (20 lb.) 49 lb.	San Luis Reservoir	Len Bearden

Now that's impressive! Every one of the world records in all tippet classes for landlocked striped bass comes from either San Luis Reservoir or the O'Neill Forebay.

All those records are owned by Al Whitehurst and Len Bearden, both dedicated and skilled anglers whose fly-angling goal was to catch world-record landlocked stripers on fly. They both knew which lakes would provide their best chances for success, and both have spent countless hours fly-fishing San Luis Reservoir and its little brother, the O'Neill Forebay—from float tubes, no less. They have obviously been successful in their quest for giant striped bass on fly.

Those are just the world records. What the record books don't show are the dozens of stripers taken on fly from these two impoundments during the past three decades that have exceeded 25 pounds, stripers that never made the record book.

There have been many other dedicated fly-rodders who have scored mammoth stripers on fly from these two impoundments, anglers like Lee Haskins, Steve Santucci, Mike Clark, and Lee Amrose to name a few. I've fished both impoundments since 1968 and have

Above: Al Whitehurst displays his world-record San Luis striped bass that weighed 54 pounds, 8 ounces and was taken from a float tube.

Left: Dave Sellers, a San Luis regular, Bogies a big striper taken in front of the Trash Racks during spring.

caught plenty of big fish on fly, ranging to more than 33 pounds. Of course there are other San Luis/O'Neill fly-rod devotees whose names I don't recall or know, anglers who have all scored Big Moes at one time or another. These lakes also provide fast action at times, with fish ranging from small schoolies to those averaging five to more than 10 pounds, often with surface flies. But, like most fisheries, this is also a place where you may go many trips without a single strike, depending upon the time of year and various conditions. It is quite probable, too, that you'll often cast daylong, making

are the largest and oldest of the "Water Plan" impoundments and accordingly provide fly-fishers with the greatest opportunity to catch a trophy striped bass on fly.

San Luis Reservoir has a swaggering 65 miles of shoreline laced with productive coves, flooded willow trees, flats, precipitous rock banks, islands, underwater shoals and mounts and a three-and-a-half-mile-long, rocked-line dam, all of which are dining rooms for striped bass of all sizes. It has two boat ramps.

Big Louie has a maximum depth of 300 feet with a full head of water. It has never been is drained so low, however, as to harm the fish populations. Also, because of its baitfish population (also pumped-in delta species)—like threadfin shad, American shad, a recently introduced Japanese smelt, Sacramento blackfish, carp minnows, delta smelt, perch, panfish species and many others,—there has never been a summer die-off of big fish due to lack of sustenance or cool water.

Water is first pumped into the O'Neill Forebay from the Delta Mendota and Highline canals. From there, it's pumped into Big Louie via massive turbine pumps (electricity is generated when water is released from the big

Above: Float-tubers score very well on both impoundments, especially when the wind is up.

Right: Action for boaters can be excellent in May and June when winds are lighter. The author displays a 30-pounder taken in May.

hundreds of tosses, without a hit until the magic time, that last half hour before having to leave the lake. Sunset—and the Gods will reward you with a fish or two; and it could be the mother of Moes.

Lake Facts

San Luis Reservoir and its equalizing basin, the O'Neill Forebay are located just two hours from either San Francisco or Sacramento or an hour and a half from San Jose, California in the arid foothills of the western slope of the San Joaquin Valley, along Highway 152 not far from the town of Los Banos. Both impoundments are part of the massive Central Valley Project—part of the California Water Plan—a system of water exporting canals that run the length of the state. Gargantuan pumps suck water from the California delta, along with striped bass eggs and larva (and just about all else that swims or lives in the delta, including aquatic vegetation and invertebrates), into the California Aqueduct where all is transported into the Central Valley and as far south as San Diego. Stripers were never stocked in San Luis Reservoir or the O'Neill Forebay until the year 2002. They got there via the water project and its canal system. For more than three decades striped bass have thrived in those canals and in the off-canal impoundments, growing to gorilla proportions. San Luis Reservoir (affectionately called "Big Louie" and the O'Neill Forebay "Little Louie") and the O'Neill Forebay

lake back into the forebay) so large a 20-pounder can be pumped through without knocking a scale off. The pipes running from the forebay under San Luis Dam are 17 1/2 feet in diameter. Storage pumping usually occurs during winter and early spring. When the pumps are filling Big Louie, the area of the inlet structure (called the Trash Racks) becomes a serious chum dispenser for the stripers and often congregates them there. Once the pumps are reversed, sending water back into the forebay

Fly Fishing California's Great Waters

and into its outlet canal, the California Aqueduct, the bass disperse throughout the lake.

The O'Neill Forebay is profoundly smaller than its big brother, with only 14 miles of shoreline and a maximum depth of around 60 feet when topped off. It also has two boat ramps. Like Big Louie, Little Louie provides what many consider to be perfect striper habitat. It has vast shallow, weedy flats with numerous channels and depressions that hold countless baitfish that attract marauding stripers. These subsurface weeds, which grow thickly to the surface at times and are pocked with open areas can be heaven for the fly-fisher tossing poppers and foam Gurglers. Float-tubers often rule here, since getting a boat into the thickest areas of this salad bowl can be difficult at times.

Little Louie also has a rock-lined dam, deep holes and channels, is rippled with humps and ridges and has two islands with moderately deep water (10 to 15 feet) surrounding them, all of which hold willing stripers. The baitfish are the same as those in Big Louie, with threadfin shad being the predominant species. The channel edges paralleling the weed flats, in water ranging from 8 to 15 feet deep are definitely places to work your flies as are the other areas mentioned.

The Seasons

High summer is not usually the most productive time of year for targeting San Luis Reservoir/O'Neill Forebay stripers on fly. It's unholy hot and the wind usually screams, turning both impoundments into something resembling the North Sea. This is not to say you can't enjoy summer action, but you'll have to pick your days when the wind doesn't howl and you'll need to fish the "magic hours"—those periods before and shortly after sunrise and the last couple hours of the day until sunset. Note: if fishing from a floating device, boat, tube, kickboat, etc., you have to be off the water by sunset. Staying out longer will result in an expensive ticket.

Historically, the most productive periods of the year range from autumn through early summer. October through February can really shine if windless, mild

Above: Ed Given of Salinas, California scores a fat "teener" from a windward shoreline.

Left: Working the O'Neill Forebay flats from a pram, a popular craft for this smaller of the two lakes.

weather prevails.On calm winterdays, the forebay has produced excellent surface and subsurface action with stripers ranging from a couple of pounds to line-busting Big Moes.

Early spring can be equally productive but normal spring winds can be maddening for boaters on both lakes. Not so with float-tubers, though. Why? Float-tubers dressed properly with good rain jackets and floatation vests, can still prevail in surly waters. They just kick out into the wind, turn their backs to the waves and cast to the mud line where clear water meets turbidity. This is when float-tubing shines, Some mighty big fish are taken in spring when windy conditions keep boaters off the water. This is not to say boaters can't shine when the wind is up. Wind speeds up to about 15 mph are about maxiumum for safety, though.

Later in May and June when the wind dies down at least a few days a week, boat anglers shine and sometimes fare considerably better because they can cover more water, faster, getting to areas not accessible to tubers and kickboaters.

My personal favorite periods are late October and November on Little Louie, and December through February and May through early July on Big Louie. I've had some sizzling action on drizzly, overcast days in December, January and February. Low light and light to moderate wind conditions make for a great bite once the fish are located. Of course the big lake can be productive during October and November too.

March and April action can excell on both lakes, especially for large fish, but, as suggested, strong winds produced by coastal fog intrusion into the rim of the southern Santa Clara and Salinas Valley foothills, often make venturing out extremely unsafe. Heed the weather warning flags/lights at the lake.

Like all fishing, however, there are no absolutes and such is the case at these two impoundments, so keep a vigilant ear tuned for word of good action any time of year.

Flats Strategies

There are flats in both San Luis Reservoir and the O'Neill Forebay but the forebay rules when it comes to acreage. Back in the late 1960s and 70s one of the most productive approaches during the spring season was to drift the Medeiros flats from the tower islands to check #13, and the flats between the tower islands and Highway 152. We'd drift with the wind across the flats using a 6-foot-long drag chain to slow the boat, casting in opposite directions if two of us were fishing. We covered a huge swath of water. If no fish were taken on the first drift, we'd move over a hundred or so feet and do it again until we scored. Once fish were located, we'd drop a brightly colored marker float made from a bleach bottle overboard and concentrate our efforts in that area until the fish left. A brisk breeze of around six mph and water not quite capping, proved better at times than dead-calm conditions. Stripers are notorious for abandoning their caution when the surface is lightly roiled and foamy. Accordingly, a light to moderate breeze can be a boon at times. Look for mudlines stirred by waves. The turbid water cloaks the attacks of stripers on baitfish seeking refuge in the mudline.

Above: The Dinosaur Point launch ramp is preferred over the Balsalt ramp by most vets.

Middle: A good depth-finder is essential to locating the best structure, and locating fish and schools of bait. Portables such as the Bottomline Buddy unit are popular with both boaters and tubers.

Opposite page: Many productive coves have willow trees that become submerged or partially submerged and these are productive areas at times; Ed Given scores a nice one from one of the tree coves.

Since those days, the flat between the islands and the highway have become a favorite with sailboarders and this makes fishing there somewhat hazardous . Weeds have also flourished, and by late spring it's often impossible to drift in the same way so you have to concentrate on working the openings in the weeds with both surface and subsurface flies. The water depth on the flats ranges from about four to eight or so feet and the fish can often be in skinny water making it a tuber's game.

A word of caution: The forebay water level rises and falls quite dramatically at times depending upon pumping schedules. Boats pulled up on shore at night are often found many yards from the water in morning since water released that night into the California Aqueduct, dropped the lake's water level. Coversely it can rise leaving your boat many yards from shore—or worse. Humps, shoals and islands once submerged deep enough

not to be boaters' hazards can become prop-busters overnight.

Working the edges of the weed flats where the water ranges from eight to 15 feet deep can also be highly effective. Boaters work slowly along the edge using an electric trolling motor for propulsion, keeping a good cast from the weed edge. Look for pockets or slots in the weeds to search with your fly or Gurgler. Also work the deeper water outside the weed zone. Tubers do the same; once fish are located, concentrate on that area, moving on when action stops. Move fast enough to cover a great deal of water quickly but not so fast that the water can't be covered thoroughly. Again, electric motors and drag chains help immensely. Some productive areas where deepwater meets the weeds: Madeiros

Fly Fishing California's Great Waters

flats; tower islands; the main deep water channel from the tower islands to the Highway 152 bridge and the San Luis Creek group campground area.

The Right Retrieve

Whether working deep or shallow, a fast erratic retrieve, a mixture of one- to two-foot-long pulls with occasional pauses to drop the fly and emulating an injured baitfish, usually works best. Start with a few fast, hard pulls to push water and to catch the fish's eye. No slow, twitchy Wolly Bugger retrieves, please!

Autumn is a great time for surface action and when working poppers and Gurglers, no one does it better than Lee Haskins. He suggests working foam Gurglers (his personal favorite topwater fly and mine too) much like you would a streamer or bucktail: erratic retrieve mixed with long and short—some slow, some fast—pulls. Make the fly dart and spit water. If a fish swirls on the fly, keep it moving with faster, shorter twitches and pulls, but don't move it ahead too fast too far. Tease it to please it. Large stripers will move for a surface fly, but most of those you'll catch will range from two to five or six pounds. Schoolies can be frustratingly size conscious and fly size often makes a profound difference over pattern or color. But like stripers everywhere, they can sometimes show a penchant for a particular color. Experiment!

Regardless of whether you're fishing shallow or deep, the use of a good depth/fish-finder to locate fish, structure, holes and drops-offs is paramount to your success. Big Louie and Little Louie devotees, tubers and boaters alike, all use them. Portable graphs/fish-finders like the Buddy series marketed by Bottomline are favorites with both tubers and boaters.

Probing the Depths

Striped bass can be taken consistently with flies to depths of about 30 or 40 feet (sometimes deeper) and still remain well within the practicality of fly-fishing. I have personally released as many as 50 to more than a hundred schoolies, along with some very large specimens, a day that were feeding at these depths. The key is to use a very fast-sinking shooting head, one that will sink a fly deep enough to give it the bends.

My favorite line for deep presentations is a shooting head, ranging from 27 to 30 feet in length, of Cortland's LC-13, lead-core line looped to a mono type shooting line. I've always been a fan of 25- to 30-pound Amnesia for deep work but recently I've discovered a great new, clear mono-type shooting line that outperforms my old favorite: Rio's new clear intermediate shooting line in .030 or .024 diameter. It handles extremely well without the usual snarls and tangles, but must be kept wet to prevent tangling on hot, dry days, particularly if it's windy. Use a stripping basket or a Fly Line Tamer (a cylindar, stand-up stripping device) with a little water in the bottom.

If you don't like shooting heads, an alternative that works exceptionally well are the new sinking lines by Rio. The DC 26 coldwater striper lines in 350, 400 are solid winners. Similar lines are also produced by Scientific Anglers, Airflo and Teeny. These specialty WF lines are now being referred to as "intergrated shooting heads". The key to deepwater success is getting down quickly and being able to throw a long cast—casts ranging from 80 to more than 100 feet. Use the countdown method to locate the strike zone. If you can find suspended bass, you can catch them consistently if you present the right fly at their level.

Before you can catch them in deep water you must find them. Begin by looking for them in the traditional places: the rocks lining the face of dams, rocky out-croppings, points and promontories. Islands, both above and below the surface, are beacons for stripers. Look for bass suspended above structure, such as rocky mounds or submerged tree tops, or below schools of primary baitfish such as shad. How do I find them? Sometimes I just use searching casts, counting the line down until a heartstopping grab tells me I've found them. But most often these days I find them with my graph/fish locator, a tool almost indispensable for locating bass, bait and structure, too. Don't leave home without one.

San Luis Reservoir's Productive Deep-water Areas

San Luis Reservoir's productive deepwater areas include the following: the aptly named "Bay of Pigs", the area where the southeast end of the dam meets the shoreline forming a large cove. This is in the "Basalt" area of San

Luis. Fish over about 25 feet of water, casting toward the rocks, and shoreline, especially mudlines; the rocks lining the 3-1/2-mile-long dam; Fisherman's Point; Goosehead Bay; Willow Point; Willow Spring Bay; Coves between Willow Spring Bay and Lone Oak Bay; Lone Oak Bay (flats are excellent here too); points and coves all the way into Portuguese Creek; Dinosaur Point bays, arms and tree lines; Romero Overlook area, islands and submerged mounts; Cottonwood Creek, Honker Bay; and many more. These areas are all productive but learning their nuances will take time and exploration and the use of a good depth/fish-finder. Remember, the lake is constantly being drawn down from late spring through summer and early fall. Lake topography is constantly changing. Underwater mounts become islands, shoreline rock piles and partially submerged trees become high and dry. And finally, always look for diving birds and breaking fish—even a couple of great blue herons fighting over territory suggests a good shoreline to try. Nothing beats time on the water, and low water is a great time to learn where the best structure is located. Mark your charts and take notes!

Safety Considerations

I've mentioned wind as being the primary consideration when it comes to safety. Another consideration boaters need to be aware of is to give tubers plenty of room. This is not to say boaters shouldn't fish in the same area but don't rush into an area tubers are working at top speed and then proceed to cut off their casting areas. The last thing any boater would want to do is run over someone in a float tube. If it's obvious there's not enough room for you, leave to find another area. Tubers should wear bright wind breakers and use highly visible tubes or kick boats. Let boaters know you're there. If a tuber is working a breakline along a weed edge and not moving and you need to motor past, do so at a safe distance and a slow speed. Use common boating sense.

Landed Locked American Shad: A Bonus

American shad in San Luis Reservoir? You bet! They've been there as long as the stripers and everything else in the lake. Remember anything that exists in the delta has been pumped into this impoundment.

During the early 1970s we were catching American shad in San Luis that exceeded 8 pounds and many of us were convinced this fishery would produce the largest American shad found anywhere. Twelve-pound shad? We'll, it didn't happen and the once-incredible fishery is now only a microbe of what it once was. I don't have the answers as to why, but I suspect it is the result of the incredibly rich biomass first established in the lake not now being what it once was; or, because there are fewer American shad being pumped into the lakes now. Still you can catch good numbers of shad during the months of May and June, and well into summer. The fish average in size from a pound to over five. Look for them waking on the surface in large schools. Quietly position your

boat or tube so a cast can be made well ahead of them, letting them find the fly. Dropping a fly close to them spooks them. Any small standard shad fly will produce results, and these fish are a hoot on light rods ranging from 4- to 7-weight. Floating and intermediate lines are best and I prefer them in shooting heads for optimum distance.

Lakes of giants? You bet! It was reported that the California Department of Fish and Game verified a 102-pound striper that was netted, weighed and released. There have been stripers weighing nearly 70 pounds taken by live minnow and jig anglers and of course Al Whitehurst's 54 1/2-pounder taken on a fly from a float tube.

I've experienced many incredible days on both of these impoundments since I first started fly-fishing them in the late 60s. Some days it was numbers, others it was a few quality fish. I recall one such session a couple of seasons ago.

It was May and Dave Sellers and Lee Haskins had located a bunch of nice fish, ranging in size from six to 20 pounds, terrorizing shad along the rocks of the San Luis Dam and over a submerged mount, not far from the Romero area. Dave and Lee scored big time using Flashtail Clousers and Lefty's Deceivers. Dave invited me to fish with him the following day.

We didn't arrive until around noon, and were on the water about 1:00 p.m. My first fish, a fat 12-pounder, came quickly on a chartreuse and white Flashtail Whistler but things slowed dramatically after that first fish. We worked the entire area and several others without further success before deciding to work the rocks of the dam east of the Trash Racks. Dave moved slowly

Above: Steve Cali works the deep, open water using a lead-core shooting head.

Left: These two great blue herons fighting over fishing territory indicates lots of bait and suggests you ought to give this shoreline a try.

along the dam using his electric motor to keep us a long cast from the Basalt boulders. We'd only been working the area about ten minutes when a wrist-jolting strike nearly yanked the rod from my grip. In fact, I let out a blood-curdling scream that nearly caused Dave to leap overboard. I'd been nursing a strained bursa and my setting the hook against a heavy fish, almost put me to my knees. I held on though and when the deed was done, I boggied a 29 1/2-pounder. She was a splendid fish with stripes as black as ink and not the normally pot-bellied Moes we've caught in the past. She was stocky but well proportioned, looking more like she came from the salt than from a lake. Her fight was all it could be on my 9-weight. It wasn't the largest striper I've taken from San Luis but it certainly was one of the best; and it won't be the last! I know there are 70-pounders swimming around in those lakes and one has my name on it—just waiting to take my fly...

Summation

When: Peak period is October through June with occasional good results during high summer, winds permitting.

Where: On either San Luis Reservoir or the O'Neill Forebay located about 15 miles from the town of Los Banos, California about one hour from San Jose, an hour and a half from either San Francisco or Sacramento.

Headquarters: Myriad motels and hotels in San Jose, Morgan Hill, Gilroy or Los Banos, check with local Chambers of Commerce.

Campgrounds: There are three campgrounds within the San Luis Recreation area that are practical for anglers. They are the Basalt Campground with 79 developed sites, the San Luis Creek Gampground with 53 developed sites and the Medeiros Campground which is unimproved. Rates for peak season around $16 a night and $12 a night non peak season. After January 1, 2001 rates will be decreased significantly, and the fee for an extra vehicle and a dog will be eliminated. For campground reservations and information call (800) 444-7275; for on-line information www.reserveamerica.com

Weather information: Twenty-four-hour weather information (800) 805-4805.

Fishing hours: You may fish from a boat, float tube or kickboat on either lake from sunrise to sunset. You may wade or fish from shore 24 hours a day.

Appropriate gear: Rods 7- to 10-weight. Sinking shooting heads ranging from type-4 sinking to lead-core heads ranging from 27 to 30 feet of Cortland's LC-13 with a mono type running line such as Rio's clear, intermediate shooting line in .030 or .024 diameter.

Other productive lines: Rio DC 26 Cold Water Striper line in 350, and 400 and similar lines by Scientific Angler, Airflo, Cortland and Teeny. For popper and Gurgler action, full, WF floaters in appropriate line weights. You can also use floating shooting heads with a coated running line but up-line at least two sizes. Leaders on sinking lines shouldn't exceed seven feet, nine feet for floating lines and test 12 to 20 pounds. Fifty-pound braided loops on the ends of all lines for facilitating leaders, shooting line and backing work best.

Useful fly patterns: Flashtail Whistlers, Flashtail Clousers, Sar-Mul-Mac and Lefty Deceiver all work well in sizes ranging from 1/0 to 4/0 for subsurface work. Top colors: chartreuse/white; red/white; white/pink/purple; white/brown and black. Standard poppers and sliders are productive and one of the best is Joe Blados' Crease Fly; foam Gurglers excel in sizes ranging from two to 3/0.

Necessary accessories: Rain gear or windbreaker, warm and cool clothes (layers), sunglasses, hat, Peterson's Stripping Guards for finger protection, sunscreen, a good portable or dash-mounted depth/fish-finder with side scanner. Float tube or kickboat if you don't have a standard boat. Electric trolling motor for you rboat.

Licenses: California fishing license with striped bass stamp required.

Guides: Prime Time on the Fly Guides service, Captain Dan Blanton, 14720 Amberwood Lane, Morgan Hill, CA 95037 (408) 778-0602

Maps/charts: Fish-n-Map CO (Lake Oroville/San Luis Reservoir) available at most tackle shops.

Nacimiento Whites

When the fish are on the spawning runs, anglers beach their boats and wade-fish.
Inset: The bald eagles are back and nesting in the canyons.

W hen you leave the lake's main body, crossing the buoy boundary into the "Narrows", it's like entering a different dimension, stepping back 50 years in time or being in another place—a northern wilderness. You quickly forget you are on a California, warmwater lake located about half way between San Jose and Los Angeles, not far from King City or Paso Robles. A lake with rural residential developments along much of its shoreline, almost everywhere except the Narrows.

The Narrows, a seven-mile canyon twisting back into Spring's emerald mountains, dotted with fragrant pines and moss-covered oaks is an incredible place, clean and wild. On any given spring morning while making the long, slow run to the inlet of the Nacimiento Rver, you might see a flock of wild turkeys, or a single, boasting gobbler, trying to impress a prospective mate, or a herd of coastal deer drinking at water's edge while a golden or bald eagle soars overhead. Canyon walls stretch skyward like metropolitan edifices, and if not fog-bound, morning sun lights up the canyon walls with brilliant hues of gold, cinnabar, tan and buff and the swirling water of the Nacimiento River coursing into the lake, sparkles in dancing sunlight.

If your timing is right, huge numbers of fish will be found aggregated in river pools and runs, young bucks splashing, chasing—competing for nuptial rights with fat, roe-laden females. No, they are not trout or salmon. They are white bass, a wonderful fly-rod quarry and Lake Nacimiento is the only lake in California where they are found. When the fish are there and conditions are right, it's not unusual to catch and release dozens a day. Much of it is sight-fishing. The whites, averaging from 1 1/2 to 3 pounds, are incredible sport on light fly rods, 4- to 7-weights.

The first white bass I ever took on a fly was while I was in the service, stationed at Fort Hood, Texas more than three decades ago. I took them from the lakes and tailraces formed by Inks and Buchanan dams on the Colorado River located not far from the towns of Copperas Cove and Lampasas. I fell in love with these scrappy game fish that hit a fly with wild abandon and fought so remarkably well. Kin to striped bass, they are even more aggressive than their much-larger brethren.

My first Nacimiento white came to hand in April of 1974 after making the run though the Narrows to the inlet runs and pools. The boat ride that first time through the winding canyon was incredibly beautiful and I fell in love with the place. If anything has changed in the 24 years following my first date with a Nacimiento white bass, it is that the area has gained more wildlife: wild turkeys, more deer and the eagles are back.

Best of all, the white bass fishing is as good as it ever was!

The Season
While some fly-fishing exists at Lake Nacimiento nearly year long, the most productive window is from early to late spring, March and April, depending upon weather, water temperature and rivers flows. The most exciting

Above: I've fly-fished Lake Nacimiento for 29 years and I still love catching those scrappy cousins of the striped bass.

Left: Boating up the "Narrows" is like stepping back in time or into a wilderness area, particularly in spring when the hills are emerald green.

angling takes place when large schools of whites gang up in the first few river runs and pools before the river is absorbed by the lake in the Narrows. As stated earlier, this is often sight-fishing if the river isn't turbid from spring storms, casting into schools, pods or just a few fish—usually a number of males encircling a fat female. While strikes can often be savage, there are many times when the fish just suck the fly off the sandy bottom and you'll need to strike at the sight of flaring of gill plates, much like you would when a trout sucks a nymph.

Other times, when the river is running higher and green, you'll blind fish, letting your shad-simulating fly swing with the current while imparting slow to medium pulls and twitches upon retrieval. Lines of choice are usually shooting heads in a variety of densities to match flow and depth requirements. It is best to weight your flies with lead wire, chain beads or lead eyes.

As alluded to earlier, the spawning period begins in early spring, usually around mid-March and often lasting well into April. Fish are not always in the pools and runs, though. They are temperature sensitive and if the water is overly cooled by freshets or freezing nights, the fish will drop back to the narrows or the main lake. Not all of the fish in the lake spawn at the same time either. There wouldn't be room. They come in waves, first staging in the Narrows or at its mouth, waiting for the right conditions and for their turn. Accordingly, you may find upon reaching the river, that there are few if any fish there, particularly if a cold front has recently passed through the area.

Even if you find a herd of fish, they may not cooperate. They might have a spawning-only mindset or they could have been fished hard a few days prior and are off the bite. I recall this happening a few springs past during my first trip of the year for Nacimiento whites.

Above: Sometimes a roll-cast is all that is needed to score.
Right: Several males surrounding and courting a large female.

Long-time friend, Ed Given and I reached the Narrows just after dawn on a brilliant morning. Frost was on the deck and lakeside foliage. Our breaths were steam and the chilled air bit at our hands and ears. I was glad we had finally reached the Narrows and the 5-mile-an-hour speed zone.

Upon reaching the first holding pool, our excitement at seeing a huge school of whites beneath the boat, almost couldn't be contained. High spirits quickly dampened though, when after an hour of passing every fly in the box by them, only produced a dozen or so fish. They had a severe case of lock jaw. Only a few days before, a few friends had experienced catching and releasing more than 75 whites each from the same run. This school was stale. We needed new fish. A decision was made to head back down into the narrows to see if we could locate a school of staging fish which might be more willing to eat.

The lake water in the Narrows is typically deep, ranging from 30 to more than 70 feet deep. There are a few flats but most of the area is comprised of cliffs and rocky, precipitous shoreline, pocked with small coves, points and some deadfall. That day we found the fish schooled in 10 to 25 feet of water along the shady side of the canyon walls. Using type-4 shooting heads with mono shooting line and leaders sporting mini Flashtail Clousers and bead-eyed marabou patterns, we clobbered the fish by casting to the banks and coves using the countdown method to locate suspended fish. At day's end, our tally was more than 200 whites caught and released. Fishing a brace of flies, we scored doubles until we lost count. A brace of white bass on a light stick is a handful. We weren't alone. Other fly-rodders were doing equally well, some from boats others from float tubes.

Getting to the Fish

There is only one way for the public to reach these fish and that is by boat. It can be difficult to get close to the spawning runs if the water is low. Waders and a hike along the river bank are often required.

High-water years usually mean you can carefully run a shallow-drafted skiff, ranging in size from 12 to 18 feet, to the first fishable pool before having to get out and walk the banks or wade the runs and pools. Some mornings find the lake in a veil of think fog and extreme care should be taken not to collide with drifting logs or submerged rocks. It's an 18-mile run back to the launch ramp and it might be impossible to do if your hull has

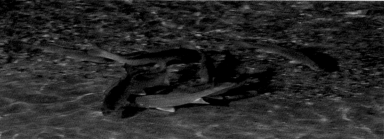

Fly Fishing California's Great Waters

been breached. Having a route marked on a GPS is good advice.

Most anglers fish from boats in the Narrows, or wade the pools and runs of the river. These days, some are fishing the Narrows from float tubes after having been transported to the area via pontoon boat. The San Luis Obispo flyfishing club has a couple of outings on the lake each season, employing this Mother Ship concept. If no fish are found in one area of the Narrows, they climb back aboard the pontoon boat and head for another, and so on until willing whites are located. It's fairly safe tubing the Narrows since the speed limit there is restricted to five miles per hour.

The Post-Spawn Period

The typical Nacimiento white bass spawning period can encompass four to six weeks, more or less, depending upon factors like water temperature. Once the major spawn is over, these now ravenous mini-stripers storm

Above and left: Ed Given fighting and displaying a fat female white bass taken in the Narrows.

the main lake, ravaging threadfin shad populations by herding them onto flats or into bays and coves so tightly the frantic shad leap onto shore, to be picked off by gulls and ravens. Fly-fishing the post-spawn feeding blitz can be an awesome experience, with exciting, non-stop action, often on top with small poppers.

That same year about three weeks after the major spawning runs were over, Ed Given and I hit Lake Nacimiento again, but were actually targeting the giant crappie which also abound in the lake. We found enough crappie for the photos we wanted, but we also found some of the fastest white bass fishing of the season in several tight coves, located in various arms of the lake.

Particularly hot was the Las Tablas arm where Ed and I found whites pushing the shad so savagely the frantic baitfish were leaping onto shore. At times, we actually cast our flies onto the bank, pulling them into the water, with strikes coming from bass feeding with their backs above water. Gulls and ravens joined the action, too, and we had to be careful not to hook a bird. In one productive cove, I made 30 casts, hooking 30 fish in succession. We could call a strike nearly at will— action angling dreams are made of.

Lake Nacimiento Bonus Species

The lake also has a large population of spotted bass, black and white crappie and smallmouth bass. It is not unusual to catch all or one or two of these species when targeting white bass.

A Little History About the Fish, and Lake Nacimiento

White bass are of the family Serranidae and are kissing cousins of the striped bass and several other species of true basses found in the eastern United States and Europe. They differ from striped bass largely by their deeper bodies and much smaller maximum size (five pounds is about tops). The species is easily recognizable by the typical horizontal black stripes along the sides and dark gray or olive-colored back blending into white on the belly.

White bass are found naturally in large river systems and in the Gulf Coast rivers from Mississippi to northern Mexico. They have been introduced into many Western waters, including those of New Mexico, Utah, Colorado, Nevada, Arizona and California. Many of the Southern states enjoy large populations of white bass.

Whites spawn in running water or over shallow areas in lakes when the temperature of the water reaches 58 to 75 degrees F. Their eggs are demersal (sinking to the bottom), indicating that a firm substrate is necessary for successful reproduction.

They feed on a variety of things, such as invertebrates and small baitfishes. A large population of forage fish, such as threadfin shad, is necessary for white bass to fare well. Waters that lack such forage yield only nominal populations, and fishing will rarely reach the point of being good. This, and suitable spawning habitat, are prime considerations when seeking waters for white bass liberation.

White bass are a pelagic species which means they utilize the deep and open water areas of lakes and rivers. Therefore, they compete little with other species that frequent the shoreline, such as large and smallmouth

Above: During the post-spawn period in June and July, voracious schools of white bass push threadfin shad into the ends of coves where non-stop action keeps fly anglers busy for hours.

Right: White bass are a handsome hard-fighting fish. They are a close cousin of the striped bass, and are often cross-bred with stripers to produce what are called "wipers" or "sunshine bass."

bass, crappie and bluegill. They are prolific, establishing themselves quickly, and are relatively easy to catch, particularly on flies.

White bass grow fairly fast, reaching a length of 4 to 6 inches their first year, 9 to 11 inches by the end of their second year, and 3-year-olds will range from 11 to 14 inches and weigh from 1 1/2 to 3 1/2 pounds. They are short-lived, rarely reaching more than five pounds.

Harold K. Chadwick and Chuck von Geldern of the inland fisheries branch, California D.G. & G. were the key personnel conducting the study which subsequently led to the stocking of white bass into Lake Nacimiento, San Luis Obispo County, on November 17, 1965.

The first planting consisted of about 160 fingerlings

from four to six inches which came from Lake McConaughy, a reservoir in Keith County, Nebraska. An additional planting of 64 adults, a mix of male and females, into Nacimiento was done on February 17, 1966 near the confluence of the Nacimiento River where they were expected to spawn.

Subsequent stockings were made into the lake from Utah in 1967 and from Nevada in the summer of 1968.

The first successful spawning occurred in the spring of 1970 and a viable fishery developed in 1971. The introduced White bass successfully spawned again in both 1973 and 1974 and were here to stay.

Lake Nacimiento was chosen for the introduction of white bass because of its large size, potential spawning habitat and abundant threadfin shad population, and since it was not tributary to the California delta, the latter of which became a key management issue.

White bass can and will hybridize with striped bass in a natural environment. If the whites somehow found their way into the California delta, cross-breeding would lead to the extinction of both

Fly Fishing California's Great Waters

species since the resulting hybrids would be sterile.

Problems arose when zealous white bass devotees started illegally transporting white bass to other California waters, some that were tributary to the delta. Those waters had to be eradicated of white bass. Today you are not allowed to have a live white bass in your possession and any you intend to keep for food must be instantly killed. The bag limit for Nacimiento white bass, once only five fish in the mid-70s, is now unlimited. They are thriving, despite there being no bag limit, and each year when water conditions are conducive,

successful spawning keeps the Nacimiento white bass fishery alive and well.

Chuck von Geldern once felt that white bass in California would only be a passing novelty for most Californians. Today some biologists wish they were never introduced here because of the delta concern. Well, I for one, am pleased they are here; and, while I certainly can't speak for others, as far as I'm concerned they are no passing infatuation with me. I can't wait to get another crack at those scrappy Nacimiento whites this spring.

Planning a Trip

Getting There

Lake Nacimiento is located 17 miles northeast of Paso Robles, California and is about 2 1/2 hours from the San Jose—San Francisco peninsula. Take Highway 101 to the Bradly turnoff, heading west about a 1/4 mile to Nacimiento Road which leads to Lake Nacimiento Resort and the marina.

The resort has every facility and service that you might need and information about the lake and current fishing reports can be had by calling (805) 238-1056.

For information about camping and other lodge at (805) 238-3256, or go online at www.nacimientresort.com.

Tackle & Flies

If you have trout gear, you have what it takes to fly-fish for white bass, in most circumstances. Four- to 7-weight rods, 8 1/2 to 9 feet in length, are perfect, with a 6- or even 7-weight being best if you have to toss larger flies with heavier sinking lines. Many anglers, such as Ed Given, prefer to fish a brace of flies, usually of different size and color, and the beefier lines and rods make the job of casting them easier.

Reels need not have a stout drag since most of the fish will be hand-played. The average-sized trout fly reel will suffice.

Fly lines may vary, but most Nacimiento anglers prefer shooting heads of varying density. A floater or intermediate for the shallow, spawning runs and type-3 to -6 sinking heads for deeper pools, the Narrows, and in the various main-body coves. Of course, you may use full-length sinkers and floaters, sink-tips and the newer integrated shooting heads made so popular by Jim Teeny and Rio. But remember, these will not afford you the same versatility as shooting heads.

Single-strand, mono shooting line, such as Amnesia, or Rio's clear intermediate in .030 or .024 diameter or a small-diameter, coated shooting line will suffice when tossing heads. Mono allows deeper presentations and greater distance with lighter rods.

Leaders

Unless the water is gin-clear in the spawning runs and pools, you can get by with a leader from 7 to 10 feet in length, with a tippet ranging from 6 to 10 pounds. I usually fish 8-pound in the Narrows and main lake.

Flies

My personal favorite pattern is a size-4 to -2 SPS (Shad/Perch Simulator) Flashtail Clouser with small, chrome lead eyes or Spirit River I-Balz, silver Flashabou flashtail and silver Flashabou side flash, tied on an Eagle Claw 413 60-degree bend jig hook. The wing is white calf tail, topped with hot pink calf tail or bucktail, followed by purple bucktail and puple Krystal Flash. This pattern catches everything from bluegill to steelhead and stripers, and is one of the deadliest white bass patterns. The same fly in chartreuse/white is also productive. My second favorite syle is a rabbit-strip Clouser, same hook, eyes, size and colors.

Ed Given likes the SPS Flashtail Clouser as well, but also fishes a size-6 to -2 pattern with a white or yellow marabou tail, white or yellow chenille body, silver rib, with blue or green Flashabou over the tail and back, shrimp style. The fly has silver beadchain eyes and is weighted with wraps of lead wire.

Almost any shad-style fly with a marabou tail will work well on whites; and, at times, particularly when the water is clear, a size-10 Green Comet with silver body is killer.

The overall length of any white bass fly for Lake Nacimiento, shouldn't exceed two-and-a-half inches.

Retrieval Techniques

Regardless of the fly, the best retrieval pattern seems to be a mix of short to medium length, slow pulls, mixed with short twitches, stops and drops. A teasing retrieve that is varied. In the riffles and pools, the fly is often fished plowing the sandy bottom and takes are more visual than felt. In the Narrows, the fish tend to hit hard and takes are easily detected.

CHAPTER 10

Fall River Valley:

Trout Opportunities From a Fast Boat

The docks at Lava Creek Lodge where I docked my 18-foot Western Eagle Skiff, not exactly a classical trout-fishing boat, but a type that works extremely well covering the extensive river and springs system.

Inset: One of several beautiful rainbows the author caught and released while fishing the Little Tule River.

It was June 2001 and it had been a decade or more since I last fished Northern California's incredible Fall River and then it was the upper section. I had a splendid time sharing a john boat with Bill Langston while my wife, Cindy and Bill's wife, Bev, scoured the Fall River Valley for Indian arrow heads and other collectibles. Fishing was fair but I sensed this section of river had seen its hey days, for whatever reason.

I hadn't given Fall River a second thought (I didn't know what I was missing) until a couple of years ago when old friends like Frank Bertaina and Leon Pimentel started tantalizing my angling sensitivities with tales of big fish and fast fly-fishing on the lower Fall River, Little Tule River, Big Tule River, Eastman Lake and in the seclusive "Ahjumawi Lava Springs" where sight-fishing to trophy rainbows was akin to stalking huge bonefish on a pristine tropical flat and every bit as challenging. The final straw was when Frank mentioned that much of the fishing for the Moes involved pulling streamers, the likes of Matukas. I love streamer fishing for big trout. It's the grab! Makes me shudder just thinking about it! The fact that Leon Pimentel scored a monster 10-pound-plus rainbow from the "Springs" on a size-four olive Matuka had nothing to do with stoking my fire for a return trip to the Fall River Valley. Honest!

Frank Bertaina, at the time part owner and Manager of Lava Creek Lodge, located on the shore of Eastman Lake, has been fishing the above-mentioned waters for decades. When it comes to local knowledge, Frank is tough to beat and he is incredibly willing to share that knowledge. It was Frank who finally talked me and Cindy into spending a week up at Lava Creek Lodge in June 2001.

Frank was adamant about my bringing up a boat and when I asked if he meant my pram, he replied "Hell, no! Haul up your skiff!" He was dead serious. I trailered up Prime Time II, my 18-foot, center console Western Eagle skiff powered by a hundred horses. I couldn't help but think "overkill" but I was I dead wrong. I soon realized what Frank knew well: a fast boat is a huge advantage when plying the lower reaches of Fall River, Little and Big Tule rivers, Eastman Lake and the Springs. There is an incredible amount of productive water with endless, diverse opportunities. Getting to all of it quickly makes a huge difference. No, a pram with a small outboard or an electric pusher just won't do—not if you intend on maximizing your flyfishing opportunities.

Now this doesn't mean you have to have a big boat hung with a whopper motor. Something ranging from 10 to 16 feet pushed by 15 to 40 or so horses will suffice. But if you happen to have a skiff like mine or something similar, that's even better.

Noted, there are also some opportunities on Eastman Lake and the upper portions of Little Tule River that can be experienced from a pram, canoe or kayak, but your range and opportunities will be severely limited.

Fast Boats, Fishing Areas: Further Clarification

There is controversy regarding gas-powered motors on the slow-motoring sections of Fall River, and I believe

Above: Rowing carefully across one of the spring holes where huge trout can be seen scurrying away.

Left: Jon boats with a moderate-sized motor and an electric trolling motor are more than adequate to cover the waters of the Fall River Valley.

some clarification regarding the scope of this chapter is prudent.

I don't know all the issues, but pollution from gas/oil and bank erosion from boat wakes are at least two of the major concerns regarding boating within the slow, five mph zone on Fall River. Currently, you are permitted to use a gas-powered motor within the restricted-speed zone but you must adhere to the limit. Other issues have nothing to do with pollution or erosion but touch on esthetics—peace and quiet—and to the safety of those

June, a good flow entered the lake and I positioned my boat right on the current seam a hundred feet below the inlet. Using a type-four sinking shooting head looped to a clear, intermediate shooting line, I fan-casted across the inlet current, fishing both shallow and deep, stripping Buggers, streamers, leeches and various nymphs. I only had time to fish the inlet a couple of times for about an hour and a half each time, but both sessions produced several rainbows and rainbow/hybrids that ranged from 12 to more than 20 inches. In fact, I managed three good fish exceeding the 20-inch mark all on streamers and bucktails—Matuka, Fatal Attraction and a large white

Above: Eastman Lake reflecting snow-capped Mt. Shasta.

Right: Excellent fishing is only minutes from the docks at Lava Creek Lodge—sometimes right in front of them.

using small craft—boats, canoes, kayaks, kick boats or tubes. I'm not going to try to address these issues since this is not about using a fast boat in the slow zone/Cal-Trout area of Fall River. It deals strictly with the lower mile or two, of the slow zone before its junction with the main stem of Fall River, the main branch of Fall River itself, Little Tule and Big Tule rivers, Eastman Lake and the Springs. I personally discourage taking a large, fast power boat into the popular Cal-Trout area and farther up river. Even on the lower reaches I urge caution and concern for other boaters. This said, let's move on to those great flyfishing opportunities I've been alluding to.

Eastman Lake

Eastman Lake, sitting under the splendor of snow-capped Mt. Shasta, boasts a trophy-trout fishery all its own. This is probably the most urban of all the Fall River Valley's trout fisheries because of the many beautiful homes built along its shore. It is fed by Lava Creek, a wondrous wild-trout prodigy in its own right, but inaccessible to the average angler because it's under private ownership.

Just minutes from Lava Greek Lodge (LCL), Lava Creek spills into Eastman Lake and the influx provides sustenance and habitat for many trout, including some broad-shouldered specimens. When I was there that

bunny strip. Most of the grabs occurred just as the fly started to straighten and were arm-jolting. Some slammed the fly as it was darted back, right on the seam where still waters rubbed currents. Long-time friend, Tooch Colombo joined me for one session and he landed a dozen good fish on a marabou-wing nymph. It was sort of nondescript but it kicked butt.

Another productive area known for large trout is along the private docks between LCL and the inlet. The water there drops off quickly to around 15 or so feet and big trout cruise the breakline looking for sculpin and other baitfish. Some monsters have been taken on sculpin patterns worked along this shore using sinking lines, from Teeny-types to standard shooting heads in sink rates ranging from two to four. Across the lake on the opposite shore is another series of private docks and this area also produces big trout.

Eastman Lake is popular with bait and gear anglers, including trollers, but it is also a great piece of water for fly-anglers looking to score a trophy trout. Indeed, there is much more for me to learn about the lake but the areas mentioned are superb places to start.

The Little Tule River originates from Eastman Lake and runs a short course to its confluence with the Big Tule River. Frank Bertaina introduced me to some of its most productive sections which quickly became among my favorites. Just a few minutes down river from

Eastman Lake, on the right bank heading down, is a large wooden home, resplendent with huge picture windows. From this easily recognized landmark, downstream to the old, dilapidated wooden bridge, is some of the most productive water for pulling sculpin, leech, damsel and Bugger patterns. The left bank was the most productive but good fish were constantly rising along both banks. The tact was to position the boat a long cast from the bank and then blind cast while moving slowly down river using a drag chain and electric motor to control the boat. Dropping the fly a few feet out from the bank and then retrieving it at typical, staccato pace, with occasional pauses, produced exceptionally well. Strikes would be shattering and I busted off several Moes despite the fact I was using a 6-pound tippet. Best lines: full-length WF intermediate to type-2 sinking. I preferred shooting heads with clear intermediate shooting line. I managed several fish from this area of the Little Tule that topped 18 inches and, as stated, broke off several much larger fish.

Trout along this stretch were also rising to dries, but since I prefer ripping streamer/bucktail patterns, I never gave the top a thought. Options here are many.

I concentrated on only about a mile of shoreline, but I'm sure there's considerably more productive water on the Little Tule. The beauty of it was that during the week I had no competition along this stretch.

Ahjumawi Springs: a Wondrous Place, a Wonderful Challenge

I can say without reservation that one of the most enjoyable trouting experiences I've ever had was pursing the

Below: The author displays one of the dark-phase rainbows commonly taken during the early season from the Springs.

Right: A typical "Springs" rainbow.

wild and extremely wary rainbows and rainbow/cutthroat hybrids found cruising the crystalline waters of Ahjumawi Springs. Here the headwaters and bays of Ja-she Creek offer unique and challenging sight-fishing for fish in the 14- to 23-inch category. It is also one of the most beautiful places on earth and this alone is worth the trip into the area. My wife, Cindy, found the springs fascinating.

While crossing the main bay before entering one of three productive spring areas, I quivered at the sight of several double-digit fish cruising the flats. They looked like steelhead in a vast tidal pool or huge bonefish gliding over a placid, gin-like flat and they were just as weary. Sightings of such marvelous trout can only engender high hopes and an acute adrenaline rush. Tailing loops and dumped casts were the result until the nerves calmed.

These fish aren't easy, and long casts with long leaders and fine tippets are generally required to score consistently. Often, casts nearing full line length are needed and if you can't do that regularly with a full line, a shooting head made from an intermediate density, clear, stillwater line with a clear intermediate mono shooting line, makes the task easier. Full lines: intermediate or floaters, with the clear still water lines shining best.

Trout in the spring areas are foraging on sculpin and a variety of nymphs but sculpin patterns seem to produce best, particularly during the early and late season. As noted, they are as nervous as a bonefish in a school of barracuda and approaching and entering the springs areas requires stealth. It pays to shut down well outside and either row or electric motor in.

I followed Frank Bertaina, Ed Rice and Tom Stienstra into one of the springs during the week and photographed them scoring a few nice fish via long casts and well-manipulated Matukas and Rickards AP Leech nymphs. After shooting a few photos, I also managed a few nice fish using a Rickard's AP Leech nymph, kind of a cross

---

Below: While you are allowed to keep a limited number of trout, releasing all of your fish is highly encouraged. Matt Havelock admires a fine rainbow before releasing it.

Right: Frank Bertaina, long a Fall River Valley fly-fisher, playing a good rainbow at one of the springs.

between a leech and damsel. I returned to the springs a couple of more times during our stay and managed to score a few nice fish each time. No, I never tagged one of those giants I'd seen earlier in the week but the promise of one was always present.

Just a week prior, my friend Dave Sellers fished these springs and he agreed that the experience was one of the best he'd had in his trout-fishing career. It was the challenge of it that made it so special to him. I can't help but agree.

Big Tule and the Main Stem of Fall River

The Big Tule and the main stem of Fall River offer huge opportunities from a variety of approaches from superb dry-fly fishing to dredging deep holes with full-sinking lines and shooting heads. In fact, Jack Mason, a long-time Fall River fan who owns a home on Eastman Lake often forgoes the more popular Cal Trout area of Fall River in favor of the lower main stem when the famous Hex hatch occurs. There are plenty of great Hex flats on the lower river that can be plied without a crowd. I didn't fish this region during the Hex hatch but I did experience excellent results when working deep holes with sinking heads, swimming leeches, Buggers, marabou, wiggle-tail Zug Bugs and Matukas.

I'd anchor at the top of a deep hole first located with my graph and then work it thoroughly with a type-3 or -4 sinking head. Many good fish were brought to hand and many were busted off for a variety of reasons but mostly from overzealous hook-setting.

Excellent bank casting, such as that described earlier on the Little Tule, exists the entire length of Big Tule and the main stem of the Fall. Of course midday action on dries can be had here too. With a fast boat, all of this water, or at least most of it can be explored in a single day.

The Famous Hex Hatch on the Slow Zone

In the company of Frank Bertaina, Ben Taylor, Ed Rice and Tom Stienstra, fishing from two different boats, I experienced some typically great Hex-hatch action during the magic hours. We employed dries, cripples, emergers and swimming emergers on the lower mile of Fall River's slow zone. Several nice fish were taken on big dry Hex patterns but the fastest action came by fishing a swimming emerger nymph with an unusual retrieval technique developed by Frank Bertaina. It outfished the other approaches by a marked degree and quickly became my personal favorite game.

Ripping the Nymph

Frank has developed a size-six, charcoal gray, marabou Hex emerger nymph that sports a simple foam wing case. It sort of looks like a Marabou Leech but with a gray partridge hackle and a bright yellow, foam wing case. Cast the nymph to the bank and using a fast retrieve, not unlike one used for striped bass, the nymph

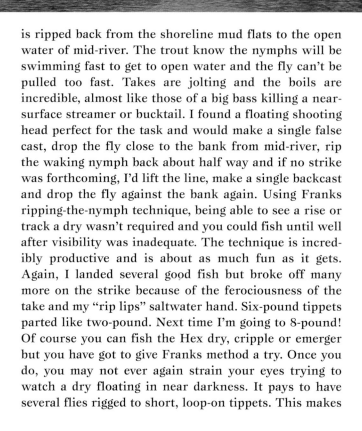

is ripped back from the shoreline mud flats to the open water of mid-river. The trout know the nymphs will be swimming fast to get to open water and the fly can't be pulled too fast. Takes are jolting and the boils are incredible, almost like those of a big bass killing a near-surface streamer or bucktail. I found a floating shooting head perfect for the task and would make a single false cast, drop the fly close to the bank from mid-river, rip the waking nymph back about half way and if no strike was forthcoming, I'd lift the line, make a single backcast and drop the fly against the bank again. Using Franks ripping-the-nymph technique, being able to see a rise or track a dry wasn't required and you could fish until well after visibility was inadequate. The technique is incredibly productive and is about as much fun as it gets. Again, I landed several good fish but broke off many more on the strike because of the ferociousness of the take and my "rip lips" saltwater hand. Six-pound tippets parted like two-pound. Next time I'm going to 8-pound! Of course you can fish the Hex dry, cripple or emerger but you have got to give Franks method a try. Once you do, you may not ever again strain your eyes trying to watch a dry floating in near darkness. It pays to have several flies rigged to short, loop-on tippets. This makes

Above: Matt Havelock displays a brilliant rainbow taken from the Big Tule River.

Above left: Anglers working the lower system where good action on dries or subsurface patterns can easily be found—the choice is yours.

having to tie on a new fly after a break-off in the dark a breeze.

Indeed, the Fall River Valley offers incredible opportunity and diversity for an angler fishing from a fast boat, spring, summer and fall. Next time you head for this region, you might want to tow-up your bay/delta skiff and take advantage of this wondrous Fall River Valley action. This area is truly one of California's great waters.

Must-Have Flies

1. Tan Paradun, size 16
2. Pale olive Quigley Cripple, size 18.
3. Wiggle Marabou Tail Zug Bug, size 14 & 16.
4. P.T. nymphs, size 16 & 18.
5. Rickard AP Leech Nymph, size 8
6. Muddy bronze Matuka, size 6
7. Z-wing caddis & dark olive caddis pupae, size 16

Hex Time

1. Cockroft Cripple, size 6
2. Charcoal Maribou Swimming Emerger, size 6

Tackle

Rods: Should range from 4- to 6-weight with a 7-weight for tossing larger, weighted flies.
Lines: Full-length WF floaters and sinkers, intermediate to type 4. Shooting heads in the same densities are also desirable.
Leaders: Typical leaders for spring-creek dry-fly presentations. For streamer and Bugger work, leaders need not be as long or as delicate. When ripping the Hex swimming emerger, a stout tippet is required.
Reels: Any good trout reel with adequate drag and line capacity.

Spring Fever Shad

American shad are often called the "poor man's tarpon" since they pull hard and often jump.
Inset: They are a favorite spring fly-rod quarry for both young and old, beginner to seasoned vet.

*S*pring Fever likely strikes fly-fishers as hard or harder than most, particularly those who spend many dreary winter days tying flies instead of casting them to a favorite quarry. Of course the best cure for a severe dose of Spring Fever is the arrival of spring itself, accompanied by several hours—or better, days— of good fly-fishing. For many, the first fish of spring may be trout, panfish or bass; or, for those inhabiting Northern California, it could be the American shad, a spunky anadromous species that ascend certain coastal watercourses each spring, often in such great numbers the runs are referred to as the Silver Hoard. For many, fly-rodding for shad is the best prescription for treating a serious case of Spring Fever.

The American shad has been likened to many species in terms of sporting quality. They have often been referred to as the Poor Man's Tarpon, or Poor Man's salmon or steelhead, for example. Truthfully, on a one-to-one comparison, a shad couldn't hold its own with any of them, except perhaps the smaller steelhead. To its credit, though, those tags come from the fact that the shad does have some of the better qualities of each. First and foremost, it readily strikes a fly, both wet and dry, and they are a handsome fish with sides flashing pearlescent, white and silver, their backs resplendent in hues of iridescent blue, green and purple. They do jump occasionally and sprint off on long, powerful runs, particularly when hooked in heavy water. Adult shad average in size from three to six pounds with occasional larger ones. Individuals from four to six pounds, which are usually females, are the toughest to handle, providing great sport when using light rods ranging in size from 6- to 8-weight. One of the wonderful aspects of shad fishing is that it's done from early spring often well into summer, depending upon locale. It is similar to winter steelhead fishing without the miseries of cold weather.

Above: American shad are a handsome fish, belonging to the herring family. Left: When American shad arrive in full force, they can carpet the river bottom.

And finally, because of their great numbers on some rivers, a fish on nearly every cast is possible at times. Of course, timing and luck are a huge part of the game. Indeed, for many, the American shad is nearly the perfect river-run fly-rod fish, for both expert and novice alike.

Here in Northern California we are blessed with many excellent shad rivers, with some of the best runs occurring in the Sacramento Valley. Banner rivers include the Sacramento River, the American River, the Feather River and the Yuba River. Other sometimes-productive shad rivers that are not part of the interior valley river system, are the Russian River, Klamath River and Trinity River.

Like all things, nothing remains the same and our shad fishing today, while still very good, isn't what it was during the heydays of the 50s and 60s. Dams, water diversions, both large and small, and improperly screened powerplant intakes, among other things, have reduced the size of our shad runs. Consequently, predicting where and when and how strong the runs will be can be difficult and quality angling varies from season to season. That said, shad migrations we still have and while fishing will probably never be like it once was, excellent sport is still available for those who do their homework and keep an ear tuned for the news that the shad are running.

the ramp at Discovery Park. Once on the river, the most productive method is to allow the fly to swing and dart in the current directly behind the boat. As a general rule, shad should be in this area around "tax time".

If the water in the American River is warm enough around April 15th, some shad will move into the lower American where they can be taken by boat anglers

Above: The confluence of the Sacramento and Feather rivers at Verona is a well-known early-season hot-spot.

Right: Both wade-fishers and boat anglers can score well, with boats having a distinct advantage.

Opposite: Just down stream from the confluence, both boat and wading anglers work the seam.

An Eastern Transplant

Like striped bass and many of our other best California game fish, American shad were introduced into our waters as a gift from the east in 1871. It began with a mere six cans of Hudson River shad fry which were liberated into the Sacramento River just below the town of Tehama. From there, the runs manifested all the way to the Columbia River system. The hub of the western shad fishery, though, is still the rivers of the Sacramento Valley.

American River

While California Department of Fish and Game studies have shown American shad to be present year 'round in the Sacramento-San Joaquin Delta, no significant sport-fishery exists until the spawning runs begin in April. First indications that the shad are moving are when gear anglers start taking them at the Brick Yard and the Minnow Hole on the Sacramento river, below the city of Sacramento. This can begin as early as the second week of April.

Once the Minnow Hole begins producing, start looking for action where the Sacramento and American Rivers join at Discovery Park, inside the city limits of Sacramento. I have experienced superb angling there in years past, working flies in the mud line where the clearer water of the American meets the dirty Sacramento. The fish seem to hold tight along this line and here is where you'll need to swim your flies on a sinking line. The only practical way to do this, though, is while fishing from a boat. Prams and car-toppers can be launched from shore and trailered boats can utilize

working the area from the Highway 99/Interstate 5 bridge downstream to the Sacramento, a stretch of only a few hundred yards. Action at the confluence of these two rivers usually peaks by the first of May.

By mid-May, providing water flows and temperatures are to their liking, shad should show in good numbers throughout the lower stretches of the American River. While there are several good areas to try, you might want to concentrate on the Paradise Beach riffle, behind the California Exposition building near J Street and Carleson Drive, and on the riffles both up and down-stream of the Watt Avenue bridge.

June is the peak month on the American and by then shad should be finning all the way to the Nimbus Dam pool at Hazel Avenue. The majority of the fish will have migrated into the upper reaches by then and plying the riffles at Goethe Park, lower Sunrise Park and Sailor bar, a favorite location just downstsream of the Hazel Avenue Bridge is usually productive. Within this stretch of several miles, there are other productive runs with good access.

Though shad fishing in the upper regions of the American River peaks in late June and early July, good fly-fishing can continue well into August and warm, calm evenings can produce some excellent dry-fly fishing for these super herring. Talk about a hoot!

Prior to the construction of dams along the American, when the spring flows were higher and

warmer, shad entered the river in hordes, filling every run and riffle, carpeting the bottom with their undulating forms. The extent of the action anglers had then is difficult to comprehend by those who never experienced it. However, by most standards, good shad fishing still exists on the American even though the river is within sight of the Sacramento city skyline and is thereby subjected to incredible angling pressure.

The American is a multi-use recreational watercourse used by swimmers, boaters and fishers. In fact, rafting, canoeing and kayaking activities on the river can become intense during late spring and summer. The swarms of drifting craft don't usually affect fishing but if you can't tolerate casting between boats and rafts of fun-loving, beer-drinking, watergun fighting yahoos, you should confine your angling efforts to the magic hours of morning and evening.

The Sacramento River at Verona and the Feather River

A popular area for early shad fly-fishing is the confluence of the Sacramento and the Feather Rivers at Verona. Here, both wading and boat anglers can score, although boaters have a distinct advantage and some years wade-fishing is impossible or at least not productive enough to be worthwhile. Being mobile to locate the exact lanes of moving fish is a key ingredient. Some swear that migrating shad swim in single file. They further surmise that fishers working the bottom of a run catch more fish because they get the first shot at them. Well, I know for a fact that shad don't travel in single file, but they often migrate very narrow paths and being in the right place to swing a fly can mean a huge difference between success or failure—dozens of hook-ups or just a few, or worse, none. That noted, it makes more sense to fish Verona shad from a boat.

The best action in the Verona area takes place from the point where the Feather River enters the Sacramento to several hundreds yards downstream. Most fly-fishers work this area on or near the mudline, and depending upon the flow, areas just above the points of several rocky wing dams can produce outstanding results at times. An added bonus, which is not all that uncommon, is hooking a striped bass that can range in size from a schoolie to a big Moe.

Start looking for shad in the Verona region beginning around the second week of April, with fish usually always being present from about the 15th through the first or second week of May. I've enjoyed some very fast action at Verona over the years. Because of the area's popularity and since it is one of the first regions to hold shad, it pays to be on the water early in order to secure a spot in the "bucket". There are good facilities at Verona with the Verona Marina, campground and store providing basic needs.

By mid-May, the shad have generally moved throughout the lower stretches of the Feather and good fly-fishing can be found at Shanghai Bend, a few miles below the adjacent towns of Yuba City and Marysville. While some anglers wade-fish at Shanghai, it can be dangerous and caution is advised. Again, fly-fishing from a boat is the best approach for this riffle. The confluence of the Yuba and Feathers rivers just below the Yuba City/Marysville bridge can also be productive at times. Boats can be launched in Yuba City at the Yuba-Sutter boat dock off Second Street by the county airport.

By Memorial Day and on through June, the upper reaches of the Feather River from Gridley to the Thermalito Afterbay, below the town of Oroville, can provide excellent shad fishing. This is a favorite area with many anglers, with several good wading areas located between Vance Avenue and Palm Avenue, which are off Larkin Avenue near the small community of East Biggs, not far from Gridley.

This stretch of river is part of a federal wildlife refuge and easy access is available along both banks. While there are good wading areas and places where shore anglers can score well, it is advisable to also have a small car-topper or pram for working the river from Vance Avenue up to the Thermalito Afterbay. Currents are strong here, requiring an outboard. Boat fishing this area is often the only way to score consistently particularly when they stack up at the afterbay outflow, which is as far as they can migrate upriver.

Camping is permitted along this stretch of the Feather River but there are no improved facilities.

Yuba River

The Yuba River was once my favorite of all shad waters and I feel fortunate to have fished it during the boom days when anglers boasted of hooking a hundred shad a day. Those were the times when I'd stand on a high bank and observe literally thousands of shad shouldering each other from bank to bank and riffle to riffle. During the 50s and 60s, before Bullard's Bar Dam, the water ran greener and warmer in the Yuba and flows were consistent—and the shad hit all day. The best runs were at Simpson Lane on the lower river, near the town of Marysville. Farther upriver, the riffles at Walnut Avenue were always productive, and the runs from Daguerre Point diversion dam downstream through the Hamonton gold fields were as good as you could find anywhere. It was glorious fly-fishing for shad and I spent many seasons curing my Spring Fever there.

Today, these same riffles are still the best on the river when the shad are there. However, water diversions for agricultural purposes, coupled with erratic water releases from Bullard's Bar Dam make constantly good fishing impossible. Action can be furious one day, turning completely off the next. To make matters worse, access to the river has become more difficult and it is next to impossible to gain access to the riffles bordering the Hamonton gold fields. Fishing from Daguerre Point downstream to Walnut Avenue is limited to those who have received special permission to trespass. Many anglers are now using jetsleds or are hiring jet sled guide services to reach the most productive shad beats.

Depending upon water and weather conditions (the warmer the better), the Yuba can still shine. Look for fish to start showing up in good numbers at Simpson Lane around the second week of May, and be throughout the entire river by June, with superb angling sometimes lasting well into July.

Sacramento River

The main stem of the Sacramento River from above the town of Colusa to the Redbluff diversion dam, a considerable distance, offers many excellent riffles and runs for both the wader and boater in search of shad. Working upriver, Princeton Bar is the first popular run worth trying. It is located just a mile or so outside the small town of Princeton, which is just southeast of Willow and northeast of Delevan. This bar extends for hundreds of yards and is popular with wade fishers.

The Chico area of the Sacramento also features a couple of outstanding shad runs. The first is the riffle at Ord Ferry, off Ord Ferry Road, just a few miles southwest of Chico. The second is a spot referred to as "Washout Bar" by locals and is about two miles southwest of Chico off River Road, south of the Highway 32 junction. Washout Riffle is highly touted as one of the best shad runs on the river but like all rivers, things change yearly and each season deals us a new hand. Camping facilities are located nearby.

Above: Fast action on the Sacramento River produces a nice stringer for those who like to smoke shad fillets, pickle them, eat the roe—or all three.

Right: Having a selection of flies in varied colors and sizes pays off.

Left: It pays to get out there early to be able to anchor in a hot spot. Some swear the fish swim single file and just letting the fly "soak" straight below the boat is often the best tactic.

Below: Action from a boat on the Feather River a short distance below the Thermalito Afterbay.

Next is the well-known Woodson Bridge State Recreation Area, located off Road A9, southeast of Corning. There are a series of productive bars and riffles both upstream and downstream of the bridge; however, while good water can be reached by walking to it, some of the better stretches of river can only be accessed by boat. Therefore, if you plan on fishing this area it is advisable to bring along a small, outboard-powered boat to be used as transportation from one riffle to another.

The town of Tehama, the well-spring of western American shad, hosts several excellent shad riffles too. Begin downstream of the Road A8 bridge; there you'll find plenty of good water through which to swing your flies.

The final area of the Sacramento worth mentioning is at and below the Red Bluff diversion dam, located in the city of Red Bluff. Superb shad fishing can be found from just below the dam to several miles downstream of it. Most of the fishing here requires a boat with a good motor since the currents can often be brisk. Shad begin to stack up in this region because it is the extreme end of their spawning range, being blocked from farther upstream migration by the Red Bluff diversion dam, despite the fact there is a fish ladder provided. Shad will rarely ascend a fish ladder. There are good camping and launching facilities here, making this a superb area for anglers to focus on, particularly late in the season.

The entire stretch of the Sacramento River, from Princeton to Red Bluff, will normally hold shad by Memorial Day weekend, with the runs peaking in late June. However, I've experienced great fishing throughout July in the upper reaches and have often found good fishing well into August at Red Bluff—so don't give up too soon if you're a shad-on-fly enthusiast.

Gear and Flies

Rods needn't be the big guns of fly-fishing but should range from 7- to 9-weight, since females often range larger than six pounds and can provide a serious slugfest in fast water. Don't go under-gunned. Reels should have a strong, smooth drag and lots of string because some fish will get into your backing; and, it is not unusual to hook into a whopper salmon or striped bass. I happen to like the modern "true" large-arbor reels which provide greater cranking speed.

Any river fly-fishing is a lesson in uncertainty: no one can say from season to season what the water levels and flows will be. Accordingly, it pays to carry a complete system of shooting heads ranging from floaters and slow-sinking to the very fast-sinking densities, including lead-core heads. Doing so will enable you to deal with any condition the rivers may dictate. Likewise, having a large selection of shad flies in a variety of sizes and colors is well-advised. Have some from size 10 through size two and don't be afraid to use small flies. Shad have keen eyes and have no problem spotting a tiny offering, which is what they want if the water is gin—after all, they are plankton feeders.

Got a case of Spring Fever? Cure it with a sure-fire remedy—lots of fly-fishing for American shad, one of the West's most popular fly-rod game fishes. Hey, it's May and they're in the rivers now! Get cured!

Great Flies for Great Waters

A selection of head-eyed, marabou white bass flies.
Inset: A selection of Lefty Deceivers—a great fly for just about everything.

Smith River, Chetco River King Salmon

When it comes to productive king-salmon fly patterns for the rivers of California and lower Oregon, nothing much has changed during the past 40 years. Comets and shrimp patterns in various colors and sizes still dominate the fly boxes of die-hard vets. Some new body materials like Edgebright have been put to good use on Comet styles, making bodies glow like fluorescent light bulbs when caught by sunlight in clear water. Bodies of silver or gold Diamond Braid or plain Mylar piping still take plenty of fish though, and Diamond Braid remains extremely popular. Tails of bucktail and collars of yellow, hot orange, red, black, chartreuse or a mixture of yellow/orange neck or saddle hackles are still a favorite with anglers and fish.

Above: The top three colors for the classic FT Whistler.

Upper right: A big striper taken at mid-day on a black FT Whistler.

Middle right: One of the author's favorite FT Whistler colors tied on a jig hook.

Bottom: Lee Haskin's version of a Gartside Gurgler, one of the best all-around topwater flies. It can be used for stripers, rockbass, black bass and any other species that will hit top-water.

All green or chartreuse Comets are killer at times, as are dark patterns like the Brown shrimp or an all-black Boss. The addition of Flashabou over a tail (flashtail), particularly on bright Comet styles, can often make a profound difference if the water is slightly off color.

Shrimp patterns like Horner's Brown Shrimp and its many variations are still very productive and no salmon fly-fisher should be without some in various sizes and colors, ranging from dark brown to tan, to hot orange, chartreuse or Kelly green. Tails on both Comets and shrimp patterns range in length from body-length to twice that.

Fly sizes should range from as small as size 10 for gin-like, low water to as large as a size 1 for when rivers are up and visibility is down, averaging size 6 to 2. Some should be weighted and fitted with beadchain eyes; some should be unweighted and blind for low-water periods. Cover the bases.

San Francisco Bay, California Delta, Monterey Bay, San Luis Reservoir/ O'Neill Forebay: Stripers, largemouth bass, white sea bass, rock bass, halibut, salmon

With the possible exception of squid patterns for delta stripers (although I've taken delta stripers on squid flies), all of the patterns listed below will score with all or some of the species mentioned in this section in these waters.

Above: A typical Monterey Bay rock bass that ate a Tropical Punch fly.

Top right: The Mini-FT Clouser is a top white-bass producer.

Right: A variety of leech and Woolly Bugger patterns.

84

My favorites for San Francisco Bay/Delta waters include: a variety of Flashtail (FT) Whistlers and FT Clousers; Sar-Mul-Macs and Gurglers in sizes ranging from 1/0 to 4/0. FT Whistlers are designed to push water creating a water sound wave or "wake." This fly-style is superior to all others for creating noise stripers and others can home in on.

For Monterey Bay, the same styles, plus my Punch series, Fatal Attraction, Sea Arrow Squid, Howe's Rabbit squid, Lefty's Deceivers, Sellers's SST, Mini-Hi-Ties, and a variety of small bonefish patterns get the job done as well as any others.

Lake Nacimiento White Bass

The primary forage fish for Lake Nacimiento white bass, largemouth bass, smallmouth bass and spotted bass—including big crappie—is the threadfin shad. Just about anything that resembles a threadfin shad in various stages of its life will score on all of these species. Shown throughout this chapter are a few of my personal favorites: Marabou white bass fly; mini-Flashtail Clouser and JH Rabbit Strip Clouser.

Top: A hair-head, waking streamer designed to be fished on or below the surface. It's great on rock bass.

Middle: Another great squid style: Kate Howe's Calimari Squid and a version tied on a jig hook.

Left: Joe Blados's Crease Fly, a superb surface and sub-surface fly.

Top: The addition of a flash tail made from Flashabou has profoundly improved many of the classics.

Bottom: Other productive variations of Jack Horner's Shrimp.

Fall River Valley Trout

Must-have Fall River fly patterns:
1. Tan Paradun, size 16
2. Pale olive Quigley Cripple, size 18.
3. Wiggle Marabou Tail Zug Bug, size 14 & 16.
4. P.T. Nymphs, size 16 & 18.
5. Rickard AP Leech Nymph size 8 and variety of marabou leeches and Woolly Buggers from black to various shades of brown, cinnamon and olive.

6. Muddy Bronze Matuka, size 6
7. Z-wing caddis & dark olive caddis pupae, size 16

Hex Time
1. Cockroft Cripple, size 6
2. Charcoal Marabou Swimming Emerger, size 6
3. Hex Dry, size 6 or 8

Above: Small bonefish patterns, such as these Mini-Puffs, will take surf perch.

Below: Top view of the JH Rabbit Strip Clouser is a superb lake Nacimiento fly and will work for all the species mentioned.

Central Valley Rivers American Shad

Once of the great things about fly-fishing for American shad is that they will hit just about any flashy fly with bright colors in just about any size, from 10 to 2. They are the perfect beginners' fish in every way, particularly for the neophyte fly tier. Below are some samples of productive shad patterns, flies that will produce on all of our California shad runs.

Index

AFTCO, 48
Ahjumawi Lava Springs, 71, 73
Airflo, 20
Albany Flats, 20
American shad, 38, 58, 62, 76–78, 81, 87
American Sport Fishing Association, 48
Amrose, Lee, 57
Angel Island, 19
Antioch, 37
Balboa Angling Club, 49
Basalt, 61, 63
Bass Masters Society, 30
Bay of Pigs, 62
Bearden, Len, 57
Berkley Big Game, 20, 28
Bertaina, Frank, 50, 71, 73–75
Bethel Island, 24, 29, 32, 37
Big Break, 23, 25, 32, 34
Big Fish Cove, 25
Big Tule River, 71–72, 75
Black Boss, 83
Black Point, 42
Blanton, Captain Dan,4, 21, 29, 37, 45, 63
Blanton's Punch, 45
Blakely, Tiny, 14
blue shark, 43, 52, 54–55
Blunt Point, 19
Boga Grip, 26, 48
bonito, 39, 43–44, 53
Bottom Line, 21
Brentwood, 37
Brick Yard, 18, 78
Brook Island, 18, 20
Brothers Islands, 18
Brown, Del, 44
brown shrimp, 83
Bullards Bar Dam, 78, 80
Calfed, 23
calico bass, 40
California Aqueduct, 58–60
Cali, Steve, 63
Cal-Trout, 72
Cannery Row, 44, 50
Capitola Bait & Tackle, 40, 45
Capitola Bay, 40, 50–51
Capitola Pier, 40–41, 45, 49
Capitola Wharf, 47
Castro Point, 18
Chadwick, Harold K., 69
Chatham, Russ, 14, 17, 19
Chetco River, 11, 13, 82
Chico, 80
China Basin, 17
Chuck's Bait & Tackle, 29, 37
Clark, Mike, 57
Clouser, Bob, 25, 23, 36, 41, 45, 50, 69, 84, 86–87
Cockroft Cripple, 75, 87
Columbia River, 78
Colombo, Tooch, 72
Colusa, 80
Comets, 45, 82–83
Connection Slough, 26
Cortland, 20, 28, 61, 63
Costello, Mike, 29, 37
Cottonwood Creek, 62
Crease Fly, 21, 63, 85
Cuenin, Jules, 18
Curcione, Nick, 55
Cypress Point, 18
Daguerre Point Diversion Dam, 80
Dahlberg Diver, 37
Daniels, Jack, 46

Dave Sellers SST, 85
Delta House Boat Rental, 29
Diamond Braid, 82
Discovery Park, 78
Donlon, Jim, 48
Doran, Kevin, 31, 34
Eagle Claw, 20, 69
East Biggs, 79
Eastman Lake, 71–74
Edgebright, 82
Edgley, Bob, 13–14, 44, 53, 55
Egeria densia, 24
Elkhorn Slough, 43, 55
Emeryville, 18
Fall River, 5, 70–75, 86
Fall River Valley, 5, 70–75, 86
False River, 26, 32
Fatal Attraction, 72, 85
Feather River, 77, 79
Field & Stream, 14
Fish First Guide Service, 21, 29, 37
Fisherman's Point, 62
Flashabou, 69, 83, 86
Flashtail Clouser, 41, 50, 69, 85
Fleming Point, 18
Fly Line Tamer, 37, 61
Franks Tract, 24, 25, 31–33, 37
FT Clouser, 25, 84
FT Whistler, 17–18, 20–21, 31, 35–37, 41, 44–45, 51, 62–63, 83, 85
G. Loomis, 27–28
Gartside, 28, 83
Gartside Gurgler, 83
Geib, Jack 15
Given, Ed, 14, 20–21, 42, 44, 59–60, 65–67, 69–70
Given's Barred 'N Black, 20–21
Goethe Park, 78
Goosehead Bay, 62
Grandon, Chuck, 29
Gregory, Myron, 15, 40
Gridley, 79
Gurgler, 21, 25, 28, 60, 63, 83, 84
Half Moon Bay, 48, 50
halibut, 39, 42, 44, 84
Hamonton Gold Fields, 80
Haskins, Lee, 57, 61–62
Havelock, Matt, 74–75
Herman & Helen's Marina, 29
Hex emerger nymph, 75
Hex hatch, 74–75
Hintlian, Mike, 55
Holiday Express Inn, 37
Holland Riverside Marina, 32
Honker Bay, 62
Horner's Brown Shrimp, 83
Horner, Jack, 15, 45, 83, 86
Howe, Kate, 41, 51, 85
Hubbard Marine Fish Hatchery, 48,
Hudson River, 78
International Game Fish Association, 56
Islander, 28
jack smelt, 39, 44–45, 54
Japanese smelt, 58
Ja-she Creek, 73
JH Rabbit Strip Clouser, 85, 87
Joe Blados Crease Fly, 21, 63, 85
Kent, Don, 48
King City, 64
King, Grant, 15
King Harbor Marlin Club, 49
king salmon, 11–14, 38, 82
Klamath River, 77
Kreh, Lefty, 4, 23, 28
Lake McConaughy, 68

Lake Nacimiento, 65, 67–69, 85, 87
Lake Nacimiento Resort, 69
Langston, Bill, 70
Las Tablas, 67
Latham Slough, 26
Lava Creek,70–72
Lefty's Deceiver, 21, 41, 47
Lime Point, 19
Linder, Ted, 8, 15
Little Franks Tracts, 32–33
Little Tule River, 70–72
Lone Oak Bay, 62
Los Banos, 58, 63
Lovell, Doug, 20–21, 29, 31, 37
Lovers Point, 50
Lundborge Landing, 29
mackerel, 20, 28, 39, 43–45, 53–54
mako shark, 55
Manresa, 41
Marcillac, Ed, 34
Marin Islands, 19
Marina Del Ray Anglers, 49
Marysville, 79–80
Mason, Jack, 43, 74
Matukas, 71, 74
Mederios, 60
Medin, Marty, 13
Middle River, 26
Mildred Island, 23–24, 31–32
Miller, Ben, 13
Mini-FT Clouser, 84
Mokelumne River, 26
Monterey Bay, 5, 38–51, 53, 55, 84–85
Monterey Bay Aquarium, 45
Monterey Trench, 43, 55
Moss Landing, 41–43, 55
Mt. Diablo, 23, 26
Mt. Shasta, 72
Muddy Bronze Matuka, 75, 87
Murakoshi, Jay, 45
Murakoshi, 28–29, 44–45, 51
Nacimiento River, 65, 68
Natural Bridges State Park, 40–41
Nauheim, Bob, 14
neap tide, 19, 27
Nimbus Dam, 79
Novak, Jim, 45
Ocean Resources Enhancement Hatchery, 48
Old Kaiser Pier, 41
O'Neill Forebay, 56–60, 63, 84
Oregon Department of Fish and Wildlife, 11
Outdoor Life, 14
P.T. Nymphs, 75, 87
Pacific Adventures Guide Service, 37
Pacific barracuda, 43
Pajaro River, 42, 50
pale olive Quigley Cripple, 75, 86
Paradise Cay, 19
Paradise Point Marina, 29
Paso Robles, 64, 69
Pebble Beach, 44
Perryman, Al, 13
Peterson's Stripping Guards, 21, 29, 63
Pimentel, Leo, 70–71
Leon Raymond, 48
Piper Slough, 29
Palm Avenue, 79
Pleskenas, Stan, 50
Point Molate, 18
Point Pinos, 40
Point Richmond, 18, 20

Point San Pablo, 18
Point San Quentin, 19
Point Santa Cruz, 40–42, 50
Portuguese Creek, 62
Pot Belly, 41
Potato, 26, 32
Prime Time on the Fly Guide Service, 45
Princeton, 80–81
Pro-Trim, 37
Raccoon Straits, 18
Red Bluff Diversion Dam, 81
Red Rock, 18
Redington, 27–28
Remley, Jay, 9
Rice, Ed, 74
Richardson's Bay, 19–20
Richmond Harbor, 18
Rickards AP Leech, 74–75, 86
Rio, 20, 28, 37, 41, 50, 61, 63, 69
Rio Del Mar, 41
rock bass, 38–41, 45, 84–85
Romero Overlook, 62
Russian River, 77
Russo's Marina, 29, 32, 37
Rusty Porthole, 29
Ryzanych, John, 16, 21
Sacramento blackfish, 58
Sacramento River, 25, 77–81
Sacramento Valley, 77–78
Sage, 27
Salinas, 14, 41, 59–60
Salinas River, 42
salmon, 7, 9–15, 27, 39, 42–43, 48, 53, 65, 77, 81–84
San Diego Oceans Foundation, 49
San Francisco Bay, 5, 16–19, 21–22, 28, 32, 37, 84–85
San Joaquin River, 18, 32
San Joaquin Valley, 58
San Jose, 37, 53, 58, 63–64, 69
San Luis Obispo, 67–68
San Luis Reservoir, 56–63, 84
San Rafael Bay, 18
Santa Barbara S.E.A., 49
Santa Clara, 31, 60
Santa Cruz Municipal Wharf, 40
Santa Cruz Reef, 40
Santa Cruz Small Craft Harbor, 43
Santos, Gil, 43, 47–48, 51
Sar-Mul-Mac, 7, 20–21, 28, 35, 41, 45, 51, 63
Schaadt, Bill, 9, 12–15
Scientific Anglers, 20, 28, 43, 50, 61
Sea Arrow Squid, 41, 44–45, 47, 51, 85
Sea Cliff,4 1–42
Sea Habits, 28, 37, 51
Sea World, 48
Seacliff, 41
Sellers, Dave, 57, 62, 74, 85
Server Sadik, 39
Shedd, Milt, 48–49
Sherman Island, 23, 32
Sherman Lake, 25, 311, 34
Silva, Jose, 25, 41, 50, 47
Siren, Leo, 20–21, 29, 37
Sisters Islands, 18, 21
smallmouth bass, 31, 67–68, 86

Smith River, 8, 11, 13–15, 82
Soquel Cove, 41
Soquel Point, 40–41, 46–47, 49–50
South Jetty Beach, 41–42
Southwestern Yacht Club, 49
Spanish Harbor, 40
Sport Fishing Association of California, 48
spotted bass, 67, 85
spring tide, 27
Santucci, Steve, 57
Stienstra, Tom, 74
Stockton, 29, 31–32, 37
Strawberry Point, 19
striped bass, 9, 17, 22–23, 25, 29, 37, 39, 41, 43, 47, 55–58, 61, 63, 68, 75, 78–79, 81
Sugar Barge, 27, 29, 32, 37
Summers, Lawrence, 14, 43, 53, 55
Sun Gloves, 21, 29, 37
Sunrise Park, 78
Sunset, 15–16, 22, 27, 41, 58–59, 63
Sunset Line & Twine Company, 15
surf perch,39, 44, 87
Tan Paradun, 75, 86
Taylor, Ben, 45, 75
Teeny, 20, 62–63, 69, 72
Tehama, 78, 81
Termalito Afterbay, 79, 81
threadfin shad, 24, 34–35, 58–59, 67–68, 85
thresher shark, 39, 43
Tibor, 28, 50
Tiburon Peninsula, 19
Treasure Island, 19
Trey Combs Sea Habit, 45
Trinity River, 77
Tropical Punch, 84
United Anglers of Southern California, 48–49
Valconesi, Pete, 13, 27
Valentine, Bob, 17
Vance Avenue, 79
vermillion rock bass, 41
Verona, 78–79
von Geldern, Chuck, 68–69
von Raesfeld, Bob, 39
Wallings, Terry, 13
Wertz, Steven, 49
Western Eagle skiff, 17, 70–71
white bass, 30, 65–69, 82, 85
white crappie, 67
white sea bass, 5, 39–51, 84
Whitehurst, Al, 57, 63
Whitlock, Dave, 31, 36–37
Wiggle Marabou Tail Zug Bug, 75, 86
Willow Point, 62
Willow Spring Bay, 62
Willows, 33
Wilson, Captain Brian, 17–18, 25, 30
Winston, 28
Woodson Bridge State Recreational, 81
Yamaha, 17
Yellow Bluff, 19
Yuba City, 79
Yuba River, 77, 80
Yuba-Sutter Boat Dock, 80
Zug Bug, 75, 87
Z-wing Caddis, 75, 87